Forming

Change by Grace

Workbook

by
David Takle, M.Div

This workbook has been designed as a companion to the
Forming Video course

in the *Thriving: Recover Your Life* series from
www.ThrivingRecovery.org

Forming: Change by Grace Workbook
ISBN: 978-1-935629-07-8

Published by Shepherd's House, Inc.
P.O. Box 40096
Pasadena, CA   91114
www.LifeModel.org

Forming: *Change by Grace*

Unless otherwise noted, all Scripture references are from: *The Holy Bible, New International Version®*, NIV® Copyright © 1973, 1978, 1984, 2011 by Biblica, Inc.™ Used by permission. All rights reserved worldwide.

NASB ® quotations are from: *New American Standard Bible®*, Copyright © 1960, 1962, 1963, 1968, 1971, 1972, 1973, 1975, 1977, 1995 by The Lockman Foundation, used by permission. (www.Lockman.org)

NRSV® quotations are from: *Revised Standard Version of the Bible*, copyright © 1946, 1952, and 1971 National Council of the Churches of Christ in the United States of America. Used by permission. All rights reserved.

NLT® quotations are from: *Holy Bible, New Living Translation* copyright © 1996, 2004, 2007 by Tyndale House Foundation. Used by permission of Tyndale House Publishers Inc., Carol Stream, Illinois 60188. All rights reserved.

NKJV™ quotations are from: *New King James Version*. Copyright © 1982 by Thomas Nelson, Inc. Used by permission. All rights reserved.

Cover image of ship Copyright © 2011 David Takle.
NASA image courtesy of the Image Science & Analysis Laboratory, NASA Johnson Space Center.
Images used by permission in accordance with license agreement from iStockPhoto.com.
Images used by permission in accordance with license agreement from ShutterStock.com.
Photo Credits from ShutterStock.com
Chapter 1: Jens Stolt. Chapter 2: Brian Dunne. Chapter 3: Victor Newman. Chapter 4: Yurchyks.
Chapter 5: Jaimaa. Chapter 6: Darren Baker. Chapter 7: Aragami12345s. Chapter 8: Henry Nowick.
Chapter 9: Zelfit. Chapter 10: Myotis. Chapter 11: Kiselev Andrey Valerevich. Chapter 12: Luxorphoto.

Session 4 Sailing Practice is adapted from: *Renovation of the Heart in Daily Practice* by Dallas Willard and Jan Johnson, NavPress 2006, p.143, used by permission.

Maturity Chart in Session 12 is from *The Complete Guide to Living With Men* by E. Jim Wilder, used by permission.

For further information about *Thriving: Recover Your Life* and other *Thriving* modules, please visit
www.ThrivingRecovery.org

Forming: Change by Grace

Table of Contents

Acknowledgments

In many ways, *Forming* is the result of a lifetime of seeking God and learning how to balance my part and His part so that I can be formed more and more into the image of Christ. For that reason there are far too many people and experiences involved to list all of them here. At the same time, there are a number of people who have been very directly involved in the development of this course whom I wish to thank publicly for their contributions to this work.

Throughout my seminary training, Dr. Julie Gorman at Fuller Theological Seminary did much to reshape my whole understanding of teaching as a process that goes beyond the transmission of information. If it were not for her teaching and encouragement, I might never have attempted a project such as this.

As the director of Shepherd's House, Dr. Jim Wilder provided me with the opportunity of a lifetime when he encouraged me to develop *Forming* as a module in the *Thriving: Recover Your Life* series. Never in my wildest dreams did I imagine that I would be able to develop a course like this, and especially one to be distributed by such a well-respected organization. I would also like to thank Ed Khouri for his vision and persistence in bringing this series to life.

I could not have asked for a better professional team to film and edit the *Forming* video than Desert Rock Productions, with Keith, Tim, Nathan and Jeff. Their technical expertise, artistic eye, and raw talent have contributed to this course far more than I would have thought possible. Even more, their heart for this project was a constant encouragement to me on those long days of filming.

I wish to express my deep appreciation for those at the Nazarene District Office in Arcadia, CA, who gave us time and space to film this work, especially Ed, Shay, and Jerry. I am also grateful for those who read the manuscript and helped to clean up my typos and inconsistencies. And to Jim Martini, thank you for our day on your sailboat so we could capture the sailing videos.

I would also like to thank the leadership and members of the various organizations that tested this material and provided valuable feedback that helped me to shape the course to be more helpful:

  Wendell Nelson, Sue Sather, and Mark Newhouse at Christ Community Church in Omaha, NE.
  Wilma Frederick and Barbara LaBate at River of Hope Fellowship in Clifton Park, NY.
  Ed Khouri and Steve Watson at New Life Christian Fellowship in Taylorsville, NC.
  Al Johnson at Christian Mind Renovation in Tucson, AZ.

I want to thank my wife Jan for all your encouragement and support over the years, as well as for your many contributions to the content, format, and style of this course. I am truly grateful that we have been able to share so much of this journey together. Most of all, I treasure your love and the heart you have to see what our Father is doing and to join Him in His mission to bring abundant life to us all.

Finally, my eternal gratitude to God who has woven together so many hundreds of people, events, books, and experiences to make all of this possible. It is my greatest joy to join You in making *Forming* a reality and a gift to Your people.

WHAT IS *FORMING*?

Forming is a fresh, life-giving approach to Christian growth and restoration that may be very different from what you have tried before. *Forming* is unique because instead of relying on your willpower and self-effort to bring about change in your life, you build a relationship with God that has enough substance to change you from the inside out.

Many Christians experience significant growth and change immediately following their conversion. They may discover new insights, make new friends, perhaps end a few behaviors, and learn about the Christian lifestyle. After a few years down the road, however, most Christians find themselves in a place where their growth is slowing down and discontent is setting in. They may have outgrown the resources of their church, wondered if there is more to the Christian life than they have seen, or even burned out from too much volunteer work.

What may come as a surprise to some is that *the greatest cause for this disillusionment comes from what we have been taught about living the Christian life!* For the last few hundred years, the Western Christian world has been stressing an approach to spiritual development that is heavily based on setting a high standard of behavior and then attempting to motivate people to try hard to live up to that standard. But this approach has a short life span, because it is not how true spiritual development occurs. While people are certainly capable of some levels of restraint over their inner impulses and are able to commit to doing good things they may not feel like doing, this kind of effort is a far cry from the abundant life we read about in the New Testament.

What God wants to do in His people is change them from the inside out. Instead of trying hard to do the right things and hoping our inner being will somehow catch up, God wants to first grow and change our heart so we are naturally inclined to live better. That is what we call "being *formed* into the image of Christ" (Gal.4:9). The process of deliberately engaging with God for this kind of inner transformation is called *Christian Formation*.

Forming re-introduces Christians to the means of Christian Formation so they can become the people God created them to be. *This approach to spiritual development is deeply rooted in building a relationship with God that has enough substance to actually change who we are from the inside out.* Each session has a particular focus designed to jump-start your spiritual life and help you develop greater intimacy with God. The course includes fresh, insightful teaching on how God works in us to bring about change, as well as real-time training and opportunities for participants to engage with the Spirit of God to begin the changes they need in their heart and mind.

The feedback we have received from those who have been through this course is nothing short of amazing. Many people say it is the most significant step they have ever taken in regard to their spiritual journey. We hope this will be true for you as well. As a way of introducing how incredibly different this approach really is from traditional discipleship models, we have provided a little metaphor of Rowing and Sailing.

Rowing or Sailing?

For many Christians, the spiritual life is a lot like rowing a boat. Although it may become tiring or even wearisome at times, they do their best to persist and remain as consistent as possible, often in the face of considerable difficulty. Not that they try to do this all on their own. Having attended many seminars on the value of rowing and the dangers of slacking off, they keep up their energy by attending weekly meetings and praying for the Holy Spirit to give them the strength and endurance to row well.

Of course there are setbacks. Some find themselves in an opposing current and no matter how hard they row, the boat seems to go more backward than forward. Still others could swear they were never issued both oars, and spend much of the time going in circles or switching sides to keep from getting too far off course. Most distressing of all are those who can never row for more than a few minutes at a time before becoming exhausted. No matter how much they pray, they never seem to have enough energy and may privately wonder if the Holy Spirit is holding out on them.

Sometimes those who are stronger and pulling well will call out advice on how to steer or how to hold the oars. The advice usually lands on the strugglers like an anchor, but they take a deep breath and try harder. From time to time the leaders just shake their heads and wonder why it is that so much effort is spent making so little progress.

Another Way

Imagine now a sail, full and bright, pulling each boat with all the power of the wind. The oars are gone, along with sore arms and aching backs. Instead, the travelers are learning how to catch the wind and give up the work of forward movement to something much more powerful than they could ever be. And movement it is! Waves pour off each bow, and the wakes they leave behind churn with foamy water. It's actually fun!

Oh, there are things to do, and lots more to learn. But this is so far removed from rowing, it's hard to compare the two. Even more exciting is the discovery that the wind in the sail is none other than the Holy Spirit Himself, which means the apprentice sailors are in truth witnessing the power of God and learning to engage with Him in tangible ways they never experienced as rowers. Clearly they still need to learn how to sail and align with the wind. But that is light-years from asking God to give them the strength to do all the work of rowing.

Enter Christian Formation

Forming is every bit as different from traditional models of discipleship as sailing is from rowing. Most of us have experienced the heavy weight of knowing all the things we *should* be doing and all the things we *should not* be doing, and the exhaustion of being forever behind where we think we ought to be by now. Giving more and trying harder seem to be the only alternatives we know. Many of us have virtually given up hope of becoming more of what God wants us to be, because we have no idea how to add any more to what we are already doing.

When we stop and ask what it is Christians need to do in order to grow, what do we hear? "Read your Bible, pray, and get involved in ministry." But Bible reading often feels more like doing homework than feeding the soul, and what many Christians seem to get out of it is an even stronger sense of how they are failing. Prayer is also hard, sometimes because we cannot seem to focus, and other times because we cannot figure out how to pray for help. On the one hand we feel the need to ask for forgiveness for what we can't seem to *do right*. On the other hand, when we pray for strength we are left perplexed as to why God does not make us strong enough to *get it right*. Lastly, the prospect of getting more involved in ministry is the very thing we dread: *doing more*. We keep hearing the same thing over and over: "Row harder!"

What all of these approaches have in common is the belief that *it really is up to us* to do what Christians are supposed to do, and that God's part is to provide the necessary energy to keep us going. We are more or less left with the conclusion that the only difference in "rowing" between the Old Covenant and the New Covenant is that New Testament rowers get spiritual injections to help them. This view of the Christian Life is terribly mistaken!

We need to come to grips with the fact that this approach to the Christian life has very little to do with life led by the Spirit. It is essentially life under the Law dressed up in New Testament terminology. No matter how much we try to give the Holy Spirit credit for whatever good happens under this paradigm, this whole way of proceeding is firmly rooted in our own effort, based on our own willpower and our own understanding of what we need to do in order to become better Christians.

Now as it turns out, some of us are really good rowers! Unfortunately, that adds to the illusion about this being the way to go. But quite literally, this is the world's way of achieving mastery, not the way of transformation in the Kingdom of God. All of life outside the Kingdom tells us advancement is earned, and mastery is achieved through hard work. Even human maturity is based on developmental tasks which must be practiced and learned (more on that in Session 12).

Not so when it comes to spiritual growth. Purity, wholeness, healing, and restoration of the ruined soul *result directly* from engaging with God – not in traditional one-way prayer, but from dynamic tangible interaction in which we are involved both actively and consciously. ***Instead of trying to make ourselves do more of what we think Christians ought to do, hoping it will make us into the people we were meant to be, we need God to make us into who we were meant to be so that we can do what He wants us to do.*** That's the difference between rowing and sailing!

Instead of making myself face my offender and say the words "I forgive you," what if God changed my heart *so I actually forgave him* and my mouth then expressed the care of my heart? Instead of trying hard to *act as if* I loved my enemy, what if I engaged with God in ways that changed me *so I actually loved my enemy* and my actions came out of my heart? My task then becomes a matter of lining up with the wind in my sail, rather than rowing against the current of my own heart in order to achieve an outcome I think is right.

The truth is, many Christians have given up belief in the possibility of being transformed. Feeling helpless in the face of their own mal-formed souls, they resort to *forcing* the behavior they believe Christians *ought* to portray out of obedience to God. But that amounts to picking up the oars because we never learned to sail.

Well, what if we could learn? What if you and I came to believe that God not only *can* change our hearts, He very much wants to do so? What if the biggest thing by far between our heart and our transformation is our own misinformation and insufficient training on how to engage with God in ways that bring life? What if we *can* learn how to sail? Now *that* would be Good News!

Learning to be with God, to develop a genuine relationship with God, and to engage with God for transformation is precisely what *Forming* is about – how to be formed more and more into the image of

Christ, so that the life of Christ comes out of us by virtue of who we are – **how to change from the inside out so that good comes out of us *because* of who we are and not in an effort to *override* who we are.**

Christian Formation is about learning how to receive from God what we cannot do on our own, namely, *to change our own heart to be more like His*. We learn how to feel the wind, to align with it, to be changed by it, until we find ourselves moved to places that would never have been possible by rowing alone.

We have a God who moved heaven and earth for our restoration and who is committed to restoring our souls as the first fruits of His new creation. What we need to do is to stop trying to get there by direct effort, and instead become apprentices of life, learning how to *be with* this God who transforms, and to engage with Him for our restoration. Then we will become free to be who He has designed us to be and to do what He wants us to do.

I say, "Let's go sailing!"

How to Get the Most Out of *Forming* and This Workbook

Forming is designed to be much more than another course in Christian Education. Much of this course will involve experiential learning, intended to help you engage with God in ways that will build up your relationship with Him and bring new life to your Christian journey. So please take note of the following items.

Teachings

Most sessions will include a couple of 15-20 minute video presentations designed to refresh or re-orient your understanding of certain basic principles regarding God's intentions for His people. These videos are also intended to help you get the most out of the session exercises. As you listen, jot down any ways in which the ideas presented intersect with your own life experience. The more you can personalize this material, the more you will be able to internalize it.

Exercises

Each session has one or two exercises designed to help you intentionally put into practice the things you are hearing. Please participate in each exercise as fully as possible. We will begin with some very simple exercises of quieting the soul and reflecting on spiritual matters, and proceed toward learning to hear from God and participating in inner healing prayer.

None of this requires that you divulge any personal information to others or submit to any ministry sessions or similar experiences. Most of the exercises are strictly between you and God for your own edification and experience. There will be a few small group and large group discussions, but you are free to share as much or as little as you want.

With each lesson there will be at least one exercise to be done on your own between sessions. These are very important. In order to be deliberate about how your soul is being formed, you need to set aside time for that purpose. The exercises are intended to give you some concrete ways of spending time with God in personal reflection. The more you enter into these exercises, the more you will get from the course.

Workbook Contents

The workbook has a number of features to make it easy for you to personalize this course.
- *An introduction to each session*. Whenever possible, read the first page of each session before watching the video, to orient your mind and heart to the session material.
- *A wrap up to each session*. At the end of each chapter, the author reflects on how the material has impacted his own life in a section called the "Ship's Log." We suggest reading this after each session.
- *Presentation notes*. All of the presentation material is included in bullet-point format.
- *Wide margins*. The presentation pages have wide outer margins for you to make personal notes.
- *Writing exercises*. Most exercises recommend writing out your reflections. There should be plenty of space to do that. For those of you who want to preserve a clean copy of the exercises for when you review this material in the future, please note that all of the exercises done during the sessions are duplicated at the end of the book.
- *Bibliographies* and other notes.
- *Articles*. A few longer articles and various short descriptions of issues have been included.

Forming Group Ground Rules

Throughout the *Forming* course there will be group discussions about our experiences of engaging with God. The rules below are intended to help make *Forming* a safe, healthy and healing experience for all. If you have any questions about any of them, please ask your facilitator.

- Confidentiality is a fundamental group rule. Confidentiality means that what any person in a *Forming* group shares should never be repeated by another participant outside of the group at any time – without explicit permission in advance. Please understand however that there are legal limits to confidentiality, and your facilitator may have an obligation to report to the proper authorities:
  - Anyone in immediate danger of hurting themselves, others or the property of others.
  - Child abuse or abuse of the elderly.
- Participation in all group exercises is strongly encouraged – but voluntary.
- Exercises which involve listening to God are intended for the benefit of each participant's own growth and connection to God. Participants will not engage in any prophetic ministry or act as an intermediary for any other person in the group.
- Feedback offered to others should be consistent with the instructions given with that exercise.
- Supportive active listening is always appropriate. Personal advice and criticism are not.
- If you feel your theology is being challenged more than you are comfortable with, you are welcome to discuss that with the facilitator outside of the group time. However, there will not be space for debating the content of the course during group time. Please respect the boundaries of the group for the benefit of all.
- Threats, intimidation or violence of any kind will result in immediate dismissal from group.

Since one of your facilitator's tasks is to help keep you and your group safe, they will have to respond appropriately to violations of these group ground rules. In almost all cases, you and your facilitator can resolve the issue. However, in some cases you may not be able to return to *Forming* until the problem has been addressed and resolved in a way that is appropriate – and helps keep you and your group safe.

A Note About Gender Inclusiveness and Pronouns

Due to the limitations of our language, every English author has to decide how to address the issue of inclusiveness regarding gender when using pronouns. Reading the phrase "he or she" all the time is very cumbersome, using only "he" or "she" sounds very biased in modern literature, and randomly switching between the two can be disorienting. One solution is to refer to "you" all the time, but that generally comes across as too preachy. Another approach is to use "I" and "my," but after a while that begins to sound a little too self-referenced.

Consequently, I have opted for the convention of using a "singular they" (and our), despite the fact that many grammarians still consider mixing singular and plural words in this way to be incorrect grammar. So instead of:

"When a person sets aside time to be with God, he or she needs to quiet his or her mind and focus his or her heart."

I will tend to use:

"When we set aside time to be with God, we need to quiet our mind and focus our heart."

Personally, I find this to be much more inclusive and personal at the same time. And since most people hear this kind of language all the time, and I intend to be fairly informal and quite personal in this book, most readers will have little trouble with the license I have taken with the language. I hope you will find this to be an acceptable solution.

SESSION 1 – CHANGING OUR MINDS ABOUT CHANGE
WE NEED A BETTER WAY

How does change really happen? All throughout the New Testament, the Holy Spirit paints a picture of life with God that far exceeds what most of us have known experientially. When we try to make those things a reality in our own life, we usually discover a substantial disconnect between what we see in the pages of the Bible and the life we actually have.

Most of us have been taught that in order to change we must decide what we want to be like, make a strong commitment, and then work toward our goal. One of the reasons we believe in this approach is that it actually does work for some things some of the time. Most of us are able to train ourselves to exercise regularly, to go to church every week, and many other things as well.

But most Christians also discover a great many areas of the heart that never seem to change no matter how many years they try, no matter how many times they repent, or how many times they ask for prayer. They look for hidden sins, they try to recommit, they even try to stop trying. What is the problem? The truth is we have had far too much faith in our own ability and willpower to bring about the changes we need. Oh, we pray for strength and ask God to help us, but in practice that means we believe "God helps those who are trying hard." However, as we will see later in the course, this really is _not_ the Holy Spirit's primary way of helping us.

If we are honest with ourselves, Jesus asks us to do a lot of things we actually cannot do. He tells us to love our enemies, do good to those who take advantage of us, forgive seventy times seven, and not harbor any resentment or contempt toward others. How do we follow His commands when we are unable to make our heart go along with what we are supposed to do? It is not enough to just keep repenting for our failures. There needs to be a way of becoming the kind of person who can live like this, or else Jesus' expectations of us are truly unrealistic.

It is time to ask a new set of questions and to be honest about our inability to live out the New Testament by trying hard to do the right things. This session will look at several issues:
- What does it mean to be formed by God instead of by my own effort to be a good Christian?
  How does that happen? What is my part? How is this course going to help?
  And *especially* – How is this going to be different from what I have tried in the past?

As we look at why we have so much trouble living up to the standards we see in Scripture, we will find that most discipleship models are unwittingly based on faulty assumptions which simply do not line up with how God changes lives. So while these approaches may seem to work for some people some of the time, they do not offer any lasting hope for on-going life-long transformation. That is why we need to take a fresh new look at the whole process of spiritual growth and renewal.

Our hope is that this session will truly stir your heart for more of God in your life and for more of what He wants to do in you, and renew your hope for this kind of life.

[Video: Session 1 – Part 1]

Have you ever thought ... ?
- There must be more to the Christian life.
- I really dread having my "quiet time."
- God seems like a million miles away.
- God must be disappointed in me.
- It feels like I am living a double life:
     a public Christian life and a secret life of pain, disappointment, or failure.
- It feels like no matter how hard I try, I don't seem to measure up to the standards
     I know are right and good.

Changing Our Minds About Change
- What is Christian Formation?
- Why do we need it?
- What can we expect in *Forming*?
- How can we get the most out of this experience?

Christian Formation is very different from traditional approaches to discipleship.
- Not just more information or more things to do.
- But a significantly better way to re-focus on how God changes us,
     and practice what we learn.

For many Christians, the spiritual life is a lot like rowing a boat ...
- We may get tired, but we do our best to persist, even when it is hard.
     – Go to conferences, study, get involved in ministry.
- We try to do the right things, but never get as far as we think we should
     especially when compared to the amount of effort we put into it.

And there are problems ...
- Some feel as if they were issued only one oar and keep going in circles.
     – Or less! No oars at all.
- Others find themselves rowing against the current and going more backward
     than forward.
- When we ask for help we often hear
     "Row Harder" – "Do more" – "You are not dedicated enough."

Another Way
- The wind does most of the work.
- Our job is to learn how to align the sail with the wind
     and let the wind take us places we could not get to on our own.
- Then we will see forward movement.

Forming is as Different from Traditional Discipleship as Sailing is from Rowing

Most of us have experienced the weight of knowing all the things we *should* be doing and all the things we *should not* be doing, and the exhaustion of always being behind where we think we ought to be.

Giving more and trying harder seem to be the only alternatives, despite our desperate prayers for God to provide power for our efforts.

As a result, a lot of people give up hope of becoming more of what God wants us to be, because we have no idea how to add any more to what we are already doing.

What if ...

- Instead of forcing myself to say the words: "I forgive you" ...
  - I learn how to engage with God so my heart truly forgives?
  - I could then express the forgiveness in my heart.
- Instead of acting as if I love my enemy ...
  - God would change my heart so I actually loved them?
  - I could then express the love in my heart instead of acting "as if".
- I could learn to sail?

I would then demonstrate the life of God *because* of who I am,
  not in an effort to *override* who I am.

This changes where I focus my efforts.
  My task is to learn how to let God work on my heart,
  rather than trying to do what I think is the right thing to do.

Characteristics of Rowing

Rowing is attempting to live a Christian lifestyle by direct personal effort.
- Depending on willpower to override contrary feelings and inclinations.
  (No real expectation about those inclinations ever changing.)
- Repeated cycles of repentance and re-dedication:
  Stability → Failure → Repentance → Stability.
- Discouragement over lack of growth despite our best efforts.

Characteristics of Sailing

Sailing is about participating with God to move our *inner* life forward in ways we cannot manage by our own willpower and effort.
- Deeper intimacy and trust in God.
- Scripture comes alive.
- Internal healing and growth become our normal everyday experience.
- Life is increasingly seen the way God sees it (through the eyes of heaven).

To clarify: Sailing is *not* about making life easy or pain free.

Discuss

- In what ways can you relate to rowing?
- When have you felt like you were sailing? What made the difference?
- What other reactions do you have to this metaphor?

[Video: Session 1 – Part 2]

Christian Formation Defined

We are being formed spiritually all the time, whether or not we are aware of it,
     by everything we experience, and everything we think, say, or do.
Christian Formation:
     Being intentional about the ways we are being formed,
     by engaging with God in ways that are life-changing
     so we become more and more like Jesus.

In order for this intentionality to be effective, we need to refocus several areas.

Different Goal

Instead of **trying to do** the right things ...
     we focus on **becoming** who God intended us *to be*.
For Example:
- Trying to act in loving ways vs. becoming a loving person.
- Going through the motions of forgiving, vs. developing a forgiving spirit.
- Making yourself volunteer vs. having a heart that wants to volunteer.
- Forcing your quiet time vs. becoming a person who loves to connect with God.
- Trying hard to make fruit vs. connecting to the vine so fruit results by nature.
Instead of trying to force the right things,
     we focus on becoming the kind of person from whom good things come.

Different Means for Change

Instead of expecting our effort and good works to change our heart...
     we engage with God to change our heart directly.
Pharisees were experts at "doing the right things," but look at their hearts.
According to Paul, trying to keep the Law does not change hearts (Col.2:22-23).

Different Role for the Holy Spirit

Instead of indirectly helping us *do* what we try to do *out there* ...
He is our Mentor and Guide and working directly with us and *in us* to help us
     become who we were designed to be.

Notes

Different Relationship to God

Instead of just knowing *about* God ...
- Stories about what God *used* to do.
- Trying to apply what we read and make resolutions for change (rowing).

Getting to *know* God:
- Having conversations with Him.
- Enjoying His presence with us.

Relationship is something to be experienced.
> It is not simply an arrangement or a legal standing.

Different Perspective

Instead of trying to achieve Christian growth by trying hard (Rowing) ...
> we learn to participate with what God does in us through a *Relationship*
> with Him that is substantial enough to change us (Learning to Sail).

Forming Objective #1

To better understand the process by which we are formed into the image of Christ.

Forming Objective #2

To actually experience God in substantially deeper ways.

Forming Topics

Overview of the rest of the course (by session):

Foundations for Christian Formation
- God is Relational (2)   – Developing genuine closeness to God
- Conversational Prayer (3,4)   – Learning to hear God's voice
- Change by Grace (5)   – How Grace is actually a means for change
- Engaging With God (6,7,8)   – Ways to engage with God that are life-changing

Fostering Growth and Renewal
- Renewing Our Mind (9)   – How to internalize Truth so it changes us
- Healing Our Identity (10)   – Healing from distorted self images
- Disarming Our Fear (11)   – Finding new forms of security and safety
- Two Kinds of Maturity (12)   – Integrating human and spiritual maturity

Our Hope and Calling

"In order that you may live a life worthy of the Lord and may please him in every way: bearing fruit in every good work, growing in the knowledge of God, being strengthened with all power according to his glorious might" (Col.1:9-11).

Imagine if we could learn how to engage with God to incorporate all that He wants to do in us and for us! Our lives would never be the same.

Exercise 1 – Isaiah 55 and Sailing

This passage is a beautiful, poetic message of *receiving from God what we need for life*. Since we are looking for how God can bring life to us in ways we cannot achieve on our own, this passage is very relevant.

Enter into this passage with all your heart, yearning for more of the spiritual food God has for you. Listen for God's leading as you reflect and write. Since there are no 'right' or 'wrong' answers, be as honest as you can about your thoughts and feelings as you pay attention to how these verses impact your heart and mind. Ask God for what you need to see and hear. Do not worry about writing well or only writing what you think is important. Simply begin writing as you are reading and reflecting – whatever comes to mind.

1. Read the verses below from Isaiah 55.
2. Reflect on what is God saying to you about <u>you</u>, about "<u>receiving</u>," and about <u>God's Heart for you.</u>
3. Write down the words and phrases that most capture your attention, whatever emotional reactions you have, and any longings these verses stir up in you. Do not wait until you have a well-formed response. Simply write whatever comes to mind. (This is not a test to see how well you can formulate an idea. We are practicing <u>active spiritual reflection</u>).

Isaiah 55 (selected portions)   (NRSV)

Hey, everyone who thirsts, come to the waters;
and you that have no money, come, buy and eat!
Come, buy wine and milk without money and without price.
[2] Why do you spend your money for that which is not bread,
and your labor for that which does not satisfy?
Listen carefully to me, and eat what is good, and delight yourselves in rich food.
[3] Incline your ear, and come to me; listen, so that you may live.
[10] For as the rain and the snow come down from heaven, and do not return there until they have watered
the earth, making it bring forth and sprout, giving seed to the sower and bread to the eater,
[11] so shall my word be that goes out from my mouth;
it shall not return to me empty, but it shall accomplish that which I purpose,
and succeed in the thing for which I sent it.
[12] For you shall go out in joy, and be led back in peace;
the mountains and the hills before you shall burst into song,
and all the trees of the field shall clap their hands.

(this space is for Exercise 1 – Reflecting on Isaiah 55)

Nourish yourself in the Word of god because it doesn't cost
anything. You accept this word free.

Shalom – Peace

Session 1 Sailing Practice – Isaiah's Invitation

1. Read the full article, *"Rowing or Sailing?"* at the beginning of this book.

2. Read all of Isaiah 55.

3. Based on what you have read and our first session:
    What reactions do you have to the invitations in the text? (Be as honest as possible.)
    What hope is God calling you to?
    What do you want to ask God for?

4. Spend 20-30 minutes writing out your thoughts and reactions below.

Additional Reading

Dallas Willard: *Renovation of the Heart: Putting on the Character of Christ* (NavPress: Colorado Springs) 2002

Rd

Ship's Log – Session 1

It has been quite a journey so far! Looking back over the last five decades, I need to say that God has really been at work in my life. By the time I was finishing high-school, I was already a great rower. Almost every Sunday a small group of friends and I drove to a rest home to lead a service for some of the poorest people in the county. We would lead them in a few hymns and give our testimonies, then I would preach a sermon. I served as president of our youth group for several years, and on one occasion, I even filled in for my pastor.

Throughout my young adult life I often led Bible studies, taught adult classes at church, and generally served in as many ways as I could. For many of those years, I was one of those people every pastor loves to have in his congregation, because I could always be counted on for lively discussions and serious Bible-based teaching.

But there was another side to my life that never seemed to catch up with my active church life. I had very few functional friendships, was depressed most of the time, hated some of my family members, and hated myself much of the time as well. As a father, I was fairly clueless and had very little idea what it was my children needed, although early on I was so certain that my extensive theology would make me a good parent. What I did not know at the time was that I was still suffering from my own childhood, and there was no way I could give my children what I did not have to give. For that matter, I was not much of a husband either, although I seemed to stumble on a few ideas gleaned from my mistakes.

What puzzled me most of all was that my constant study of theology and the Bible did not seem to help. In fact it seemed to make things worse, because everything I learned seemed to *widen* the gap between what I knew God wanted from me and what I saw in the mirror. I could do lots of stuff at church, and look really good on the outside, but on the inside I was dying! My heart never seemed to change. No matter how much I wanted to be different, no matter how hard I tried to be different, I could not become the person I wanted to be. Rarely was there even any movement of my heart in the right direction. The best I could say was that I was becoming less dogmatic and a lot more understanding of others who seemed to be stuck as well.

But in late 1985, God began bringing people into my life who provided glimpses of what it might look like to have the kind of life I wanted. By 1998, I could hardly keep pace with the mentors He was sending my way – through seminars, books, friends, and finally, Himself. I found healing and relief from many of the painful wounds I had been carrying around for as long as I could remember. Within a few short years, my low-grade depression had lifted, and I was experiencing more joy and hope than I had ever imagined possible.

Perhaps the most wonderful thing of all was the discovery that God wanted my restoration even more than I did, and that we can learn how to engage with Him for the changes of heart we so desperately need and cannot accomplish on our own. My greatest desire at this point is to pass along those things I have learned about how God changes lives.

David Takle
Sailor Apprentice

SESSION 2 – GOD IS RELATIONAL
BUILDING A SUBSTANTIVE RELATIONSHIP WITH GOD

"We will come to you and make our home with you" (Jn.14:23).

Deep within the heart of every child of God is an all-encompassing desire to be connected with our Heavenly Father. To know His love, to hear His voice, to feel the warmth of His arms around us – this is the reason we were saved; this is what we *know* we were made for.

Even more amazing, *this is what the Father wants, too!* He wants to share life with us, more than we could ever imagine. He wants us to know how much He loves us and how much He desires to heal and restore us.

The truth is, we sometimes talk about the love of God as if it were yesterday's news. But our Father's love is more than an idea or a godly attribute. It is as real as the chair you are sitting on. And God means for you to know and experience that love in the same way the original disciples did. Listen to how John talks about what he discovered after many years of following Jesus:

"We have come to know and have believed the love which God has for us" (1Jn.4:16).

This is what John says about his life with God – that after all he has been through, he has come to the place where *he knows that he knows* he is loved by God. And when he talks about "knowing," he is not referring to some abstract head knowledge. He has *experienced* the love of God; he *knows* he is loved, as surely as he knows there is air in the room.

Paul picks up this theme in his letter to the Ephesians, where he prays for them to be able "to grasp how wide and long and high and deep is the love of Christ, and to know this love that surpasses knowledge" (Eph.3:18-19). Because when we truly *know* how much we are loved, it opens the door to the kind of relationship with God that can change our life.

The gospel is not only about going to heaven when we die. Nor did God just save us and then leave us on our own to see how well we would do. The Good News is that God wants to have a relationship with us – to restore the relationship that was lost in the Garden of Eden. This is the <u>starting</u> point for our restoration! This relationship is not something we have to wait for until we have cleaned ourselves up.

Last session we made the point that real change comes not from trying harder but from building a relationship with God that has real substance. But in order for us to do that, we need to truly grasp the kind of relationship God has in mind. We must also be clear about who this God is we are trying to build a relationship with.

This session will focus on exactly why this relationship is so vital. In the process, we will look at how God views us and some of the ways we view God. We will also look at some of the reasons why people often find it hard to have this kind of relationship.

Notes **Discuss**

Imagine God thinking about you.

What do you assume He feels when you come to mind?[1]

[Video: Session 2 – Part 1]

God Wants a Relationship With Us

The Good News is so much more than about going to heaven when you die.

God wants a relationship with us which is strong enough to change us.

> "If anyone is in Christ, he is a new creation ... All this is from God, who reconciled us to himself ... **reconciling the world to himself** in Christ ... we implore you on Christ's behalf: Be reconciled to God" (2Cor.5:17-20).

Reconciliation is the very essence of God's mission in the world.

God created us to have a relationship with us. When we broke that relationship, He set about to restore us to Himself, so we could have the relationship He wanted to have with us in the first place. This is the gospel story.

What if we really "got" this?

Relationship is NOT the Same Thing as an Arrangement

A lot of Christians have more of an arrangement with God than a relationship.

Something like: "I will confess I have failed God, I need Him to forgive me, and that Jesus died and rose again to make this possible. In exchange, God will grant me eternal life. Then I will try to be a better person, based on my understanding of what is expected and how much I am willing to do."

Compare:

(Arrangement) A marriage of convenience to divide the workload.

(Relationship) A marriage where you love deeply and share life in every way possible, enjoying each others' presence and heart, caring about what is best for each other.

God is Present With Us

God's presence is more than a theological fact.

It is a present reality and a way of life.

• "I am with you always" (Mt.28:20).

• "I will come to you" (Jn.14).

• "Abide in me and I in you" (Jn.15).

God is *not* far away – He is closer than my next breath.

Immanuel means "God with us."

Jesus came, in part, to show us how much God wants to be with us.

He sent the Holy Spirit so He could be with us all the time.

---

1   The idea for this discussion comes from David Benner: *Surrender to Love*, p.15

God Loves Us More Than We Know

If we understood how much we are loved it would change our life.

The following passage is a prayer <u>for Christians</u>:

"And I pray that you, being rooted and established in love, may have power, together with all the saints, *to grasp* how wide and long and high and deep is *the love of Christ*, and to know this love that surpasses knowledge" (Eph.3:17-19).

Paul knew there was much more to God's love than what they had grasped so far.

God Wants Us to Live in Love

Reconciliation and relationship mean living in God's love for us.

John really emphasized this theme:

"As the Father has loved me, so have I loved you. Now remain in my love" (Jn.15:9).

"We have come to know and have believed the love which God has for us" (1Jn.4:16).

"I have made Your name known to them ... so that the love with which You loved Me may be in them, and I in them" (Jn.17:23).

This goes way beyond "I did something for you so you can go to heaven."

It's more like: "I want to give you more life than you can possibly imagine."

Living in relationship to God and in His love for us, learning how to receive it and give it away is what we were designed for.

What if we could be loved as much as we always wanted to be loved?

What if we could experience God's love day by day?

God Wants Us to Know Him

The point of reconciliation is to have a relationship and get to *know* God.

This is the real gospel message.

"Now this is eternal life: *that they may know you*, the only true God, and Jesus Christ, whom you have sent" (Jn.17:3).

"I keep asking that the God of our Lord Jesus Christ ... may give you the Spirit of wisdom and revelation *so that you may know him better* "(Eph.1:17).

There is a big difference between knowing *about* God and *knowing* God.

- Analyzing stories of others who experienced God in their lives.
    Trying to extract principles to apply to our lives.
- Or ... Learning to have the kind of relationship with God they had!

Relationship With God Changes Us

- Builds joy and peace (shalom).
- Heals our alienation and other wounds. Changes our desires.
- Restores our true identity.

Relationship with God is the basis for life-long spiritual growth and transformation. If you have ever been impacted significantly by a teacher or mentor in ways for which you are still very grateful, then you have an idea of how life-changing such a a relationship can be. Consider what it means to be in relationship with someone who loves you dearly, knows you better than you know yourself, has all the time in the world to spend with you, and knows exactly what you need each step of the way.

Appreciation

Our most natural response to God's desire for relationship is <u>gratitude</u>.

"So then, just as you received Christ Jesus as Lord, continue to live your lives in him, rooted and built up in him, strengthened in the faith as you were taught, and <u>overflowing with thankfulness</u>" (Col.2:6-7).

- Appreciation arises naturally from a life-giving, joyful relationship with God.
- Appreciation prepares our heart to be even more relational.
- Appreciation trains our heart to see more of God's goodness.

These are reasons why God has so much to say about being thankful and grateful.

Why Appreciation Matters

When people do good things for us, we very naturally have a heartfelt response which we call gratitude or appreciation. We recognize that what we received from them was a generous act of love which they did not have to do. But they did. And we are blessed by their kindness and thoughtfulness.

What's more, we feel closer to them. We know that they hold us in their heart and that we are safe in their thoughts. They are glad to be with us, they are *for* us – on our side, as it were. We are richer, not only because of what they have given to us, but because they know us and care about us.

Of course, it is possible to miss what they have done for us, or to take it lightly and dismiss it as too trivial or some kind of fluke. In that case we would do well to slow down and see the gift for what it is and our friend for who they really are. It is good for us to see their goodness as it is directed toward us.

On the other hand, if we are not used to receiving the kindness of others, we might even feel afraid or shamed by their gift. But that only means we need healing or more experience with receiving things given unconditionally. We need to learn how to receive with joy, so that we can enter into life-giving relationships where we can give and receive life freely. This is how we were designed to live.

In any case, when we stop to remember the good things God has done for us, or simply how good He is and how wonderful it is to be His child, we hold Him in our heart more dearly and bring ourselves closer to the reality of who He is. When we do this often, we train ourselves to see the goodness of the Kingdom all around us, and we train our heart to trust Him more fully with our life.

Exercise 2A – Practicing Appreciation

--- Part 1 --- Identifying Appreciation Moments (10 minutes)
This exercise will highlight the value of practicing appreciation, in and of itself.

(1) Identify 3 things in your life for which you are truly grateful. Choose things you can feel genuine appreciation for (not things for which you think you *should* feel appreciation). These do not have to be explicitly "spiritual" in nature. Here are some ideas to help stir your memories:
   • A person who has meant a great deal to you (friend, mentor, family member).
   • An experience you have had (or event you have attended) that was very rich and memorable.
   • A place you have lived (or visited) that has special meaning for you.

(2) Write out each "appreciation moment" in 3-4 sentences, stating enough to help you identify it, express the feelings you have about it, and tell why it means so much to you.

(3) Give each item on the list a name – one word or short phrase.

Example:
I still remember my first trip to the Grand Canyon and how overwhelmed I was by its beauty and grandeur. As I walked up to the edge, I was struck speechless by the immensity of it all. When I picture myself standing at the edge of the canyon, my whole body reacts and my heart goes to total wonder. I call this my *Grand Canyon Moment*.

--- Part 2 --- Sharing Appreciation with Others (6 minutes)
Pair up with one other person. Allow three minutes for each of you to share one of your appreciation moments with the other person. Be sure to go beyond your short description and include ...
   • how it impacts your mind and body to recall your appreciation moment.
   • what you were feeling a few minutes ago, prior to Part 1 of the exercise.
   • what you experienced as you wrote out your appreciation moment.

After each story, the listener can reflect back a sentence or two about how they were impacted by the other person's story.

[Video: Session 2 – Part 2]

Relationship is <u>the</u> Organizing Principle of Life

God's intention is for our lives to revolve around our connections to God and other people, and He designed us with this in mind.

This is why "Love God" and "Love one another" are the greatest commandments.

- We seek to build solid connections with God and others.
- We learn how to encourage, build up, and serve one another with joy.
- We hold relationships to be more important than problems.
- Relationship is the lens through which everything else is viewed.

People often organize their lives around other things.

  – achievement – career – accumulating – consuming – self-protection

  – pain avoidance – addictions – power – being right.

Example Issue	Organizing Principle	Tendency
Conflict	Being Right	Attack & defend
	Self-Protection	Withdraw
	Relationship	Seek to repair and restore
Vacation with Family or Friend	Career	Vacation may be expendable
	Relationship	Time together is essential

Problems Relating to God

Building a relationship with God is not always easy.

- Have you ever had doubts about God wanting to be with you?
- Have you ever felt like God was a million miles away?

Many Christians have never seriously considered that God actually wants to have a relationship with us. Others think God might want a relationship with someone else but not with them.

Distorted Ideas of Who God Is

- The Critical God:
  - He is watching our every move and mostly disapproving.
  - He may or may not be involved enough to reward or punish us.

- The Distant God:
  - He set the world in motion, sent Jesus, and then withdrew.
  - He is disconnected and uninvolved in our lives.
  - He rarely engages with people directly.
  - We are pretty much left to our own resources.

• The Demanding God:
  – You can never do enough to please Him.
  – If you knew what His will was for you, it would be way too hard to do.

See the comparison on the next page between a judicial view of God
and a relational view of God.

Where Do We Get Distorted Ideas of God?

Where do these distortions come from? How do we get them?

Good teaching and sound theology about the character of God do not prevent us
from having distorted ideas of who He is.

We can acquire these distorted ideas about God from many sources:

• Significant disappointments in life (accidents, health problems).
• Overly authoritative parents.
• The lack of a strong love bond with one or both parents.
• Lack of training in how to engage with God in ways that bring life.

Distorted ideas of God are some of the greatest barriers to developing a good
relationship with God.

After all, who wants to get close to a God who is mean or uncaring?

God's True Intentions Toward Me

There is overwhelming evidence that God wants a relationship with us:

• He planned to rescue me.

  "He chose us in him before the foundation of the world" (Eph.1:3-5).

• He lavished His grace on me.

  "In him we have redemption...the forgiveness of sins, in accordance with the
  riches of God's grace that he lavished on us" (Eph.1:7-8).

• God loves me even when I sin.

  "God demonstrates his own love for us in this:
  While we were still sinners, Christ died for us" (Rom.5:8).

• He wants to live with me.

  "The Spirit of truth is with you and will be in you. I will not leave you as orphans,
  I will come to you. On that day you will realize that I am in my Father, and you are
  in me, and I am in you" (Jn.14:16-23).

Life is not a test to see if we pass or fail.

Life is about having a relationship with God, no matter what condition we are in.

We get the relationship first, and that becomes the context for being mentored
and restored!

God is pursuing us for a relationship!

Notes

Comparing a Judicial View of God and a Relational View of God

Primarily Judicial	**Primarily Relational**
Watches from a distance (up in heaven)	He is present, abides within us
Hands out work assignments	Asks us to join Him in what He is doing
Expects us to reform ourselves	Works together with us and in us for change
Judges our behavior	Understands our weakness
Angry, demanding from us	Loving, giving to us
Gives us standards to live up to	Gives us the desire to live well
We have to earn His approval as servants	He delights in us as His children
Mostly disappointed in us	Wants to be with us
Spiritual growth from trying hard	Spiritual growth from engaging with God
Primarily about doing the right thing	Primarily about receiving and giving life
Commanding / Demanding	Mentoring / Healing / Restoring
Life is one big divine test	Life is an ever-growing experience of God
Salvation story is primarily about our sin, the punishment we deserve, and God's pardon	Salvation story is primarily about a relationship with God that was broken and is being restored

---

God Cares about Sin

This comparison in no way implies God does not care about sin. The issue is not whether He is serious about sin, but the manner in which He intends to deal with it.

Many people are convinced that God simply judges us when we fail Him. While viewing God as a harsh judge can motivate us to try to live well in order to avoid judgment, it is fundamentally <u>a fear-based orientation</u> to God that will prevent the kind of relationship with Him that we need.

The truth is, He is totally committed to removing the *causes* of sin within us through His healing presence, love, and truth. With this understanding, we are motivated to deepen our relationship with Him so that He can do in us what we cannot do for ourselves, and we can then experience the joy of ever-increasing freedom as well as the joy of our relationship with God. In this way, God's preference for relationship with us (rather than judgment) is very much concerned with eradicating sin.

So does the Bible speak of judgment? Of course. But in nearly every instance the context is in reference to people's life-long refusal to come to God. To see judgment as God's primary orientation toward us is to miss the real scope of God's heart, what He is doing in the world, and what He wants to accomplish in His people.

Exercise 2B – Appreciation Moments With God

"Let the peace of Christ rule in your hearts, to which indeed you were called in one body; **and be thankful**. Let the word of Christ richly dwell within you, with all wisdom teaching and admonishing one another with psalms and hymns and spiritual songs, singing **with thankfulness in your hearts to God**" (Col.3:15-16 NASB).

Exercise 2A was about practicing appreciation in regard to any aspect of our life.
This exercise will focus on appreciation moments with God.

1. Recall one of your appreciation moments, and allow yourself to feel appreciation for a full minute.

2. Now take a moment to remember some way you have experienced God or His goodness toward you. Try to choose something that had a significant impact on you and with which you can still reconnect emotionally. (This is not merely a cognitive exercise). This should be something quite experiential or relational in nature, and *not* a material blessing you received, such as when you got a new car or job or money (unless it was essential in some way, such as after a significant loss).
   Some examples:
   • Being aware of the greatness of God in creation (mountains, ocean, or even a local park).
   • Feeling close to God through music (example: "How Great is Our God...").
   • While reading Psalm 23 or Isaiah 55 or your favorite passage.
   • The wonder of God you feel while watching your child sleeping.
   • Experiencing a glimpse of God's goodness in someone you know or have met.
   • When you were comforted and encouraged by God at a difficult time in your life.
   • An inspired message you heard.
   • A God-breathed word spoken to you by a friend at the right time.
   • Excitement and energy you felt in an important spiritual experience.

3. When you have selected a memory:
   • Focus your mind on that experience.
   • Try to engage that memory with your heart as well as your mind. (What was it like to be there?)
   • Allow yourself to feel your appreciation for God's goodness in that experience.
   • Hold the appreciation in your heart and savor this moment with God.

4. After a few minutes, ask God if there is anything else He wants you to know about this moment. Wait a couple of minutes to see if anything else comes to mind as you reflect on your appreciation moment with God.

5. Take at least five minutes to write out your own psalm of praise and appreciation (use next page).

(this page is for writing out Exercise 2B)

Session 2 Sailing Practice – The Goodness of God

"My soul is satisfied as with a rich feast, and my mouth praises you with joyful lips when I think of you on my bed, and meditate on you in the watches of the night; for you have been my help, and in the shadow of your wings I sing for joy" (Ps.63:5-7 NRSV).

This is an excellent exercise, intended to grow our expectations of God's goodness in our lives.[2] So we would like you to practice this exercise daily, for the rest of this course. I would even challenge you to consider this to be something of an experiment in simple spiritual practices, to see what impact they can have on your heart and mind.

Every morning as you are waking up and every night as you are drifting off to sleep, focus your mind and heart to dwell on the goodness of God – His character, His love, His pursuit of you over time, and His earnest desire to become your mentor and guide through life. If you need help in bringing your whole heart into the practice, recall one of your appreciation moments to help you engage more fully. Hold that wonder and appreciation for 5-10 minutes, savoring the thoughts and feelings that come to you. If necessary, put a note next to your alarm clock to remind you.

Please note this is not meant to be purely a mental exercise. As much as possible, we encourage you to engage with your whole heart, feeling the goodness of God in your soul, and experiencing joy and gratitude very naturally as a result.

More on the Value of Gratitude and Appreciation

Expressing appreciation toward another is good for our soul. Noticing our internal response and putting words to our gratitude helps us to internalize our perceptions of the goodness God has brought into our life.

Remember that we are being formed all the time by what we experience, and how we respond or do not respond to others around us. So being deliberate about expressing the gratitude we feel is an important way of re-forming our soul in the ways of the Kingdom.

Additional Reading on Our Relational God

James Bryan Smith: *The Good and Beautiful God: Falling in Love with the God Jesus Knows* (IVP Books: Downers Grove, IL) 2009

Wayne Jacobson: *He Loves Me! Learning to Live in the Father's Affection* (Windblown Media: Newbury Park, CA) 2007

David Benner: *Surrender to Love: Discovering the Heart of Christian Spirituality* (IVP Books: Downers Grove, IL) 2003

J.B. Phillips: *Your God is Too Small* (Touchstone: New York) 1997

---

2 The idea for this exercise comes from Dallas Willard

Ship's Log – Session 2

I am surprised as I look back over my life, how many years I talked about my "relationship to God" and how Jesus was my "personal" savior. Yet other than some warm fuzzy feelings from time to time, I did not have much of a relationship at all. It was more of an understanding – that I should be very grateful for my salvation and I should do everything I could to encourage others to accept Jesus. I believed God was with me as a matter of principle, but I rarely had any sense that this was really true.

I guess I thought because I had a lot of good doctrine under my belt and because I studied hard to learn everything I could about the Bible, that meant I had a relationship with God. Every once in a while it crossed my mind that I was using this word *relationship* a little differently from how I would normally use it. Frankly, it sounded a lot like the kind of relationship I might have had with a favorite author. But since almost every Christian I knew used the word *relationship* in this way, I figured that was all a relationship with God could be. I even remember a Christian radio broadcaster who began each program by inviting his listeners to a time of *fellowship,* and I would sometimes wonder, "What kind of fellowship can I have with a prerecorded message?" Is this really how we want to use that word?

Perhaps most unsettling to me were the words of Jesus in the Gospel of John. Over and over He spoke about how He would walk with and talk with those who followed Him. He promised to never leave us as orphans (yet I often felt abandoned), that He and His Father would come to us and reveal Himself to us (yet I rarely had any sense of revelation), that we would know His voice (but I never heard it), and so on. I kept wondering what He might be talking about and whether I would ever know.

As I reflect back on it now, the phrase "relationship with God" was really a kind of euphemism my friends and I made use of, by which we meant that we knew a lot about God and would go to heaven and see Him someday. But the good news is God actually wants a real working relationship with us. More and more I see that life with God is an infinite journey, and this relationship will continue to grow for as long as we pursue it.

This connection with God has changed me in so many ways, and continues to change me. Consequently, I am aware that I still have a long way to go in my journey toward wholeness. I guess in some ways, this truth makes God's presence with me all the more precious. I need Him. And the more I get to know Him, the more I need Him. Beth Moore says that when she was a child, her parents' job was to grow her up to *leave* home, but as a child of God, He seems to be growing her up to *come* home. That's beginning to make sense to me.

So I'm really looking forward to the next session, where we will begin looking at how we can have real conversations with God. Because if we ever want to have a meaningful relationship, we are going to have to learn how to listen to Him so He can mentor us and be with us in ways that feed our soul (like it says in Isaiah 55).

David Takle
Sailor Apprentice

SESSION 3 – DEVELOPING A CONVERSATIONAL PRAYER LIFE (PART 1)
FOCUSING AND LISTENING[3]

One of the first things we learn to do as Christians is pray to God. If we are fortunate enough to have good training, we learn about different kinds of prayer, such as confession, repentance, thanksgiving, and so on. Some people find the acronym ACTS helps them pray. The letters stand for Adoration, Confession, Thanksgiving, and Supplication.

These are all good ways to pray, and they are often modeled in the Bible. But there is another form of prayer which has largely been neglected, called conversational prayer – learning to listen to the Spirit of God and having two-way conversations with Him. Now since God is spirit, our conversations with Him are different from those we have with people. But we can learn how He speaks to us, and thereby experience many of the things promised to us in the New Testament.

Jesus Himself said He only spoke what was given to Him by His Father. He also told His disciples they would have a similar relationship with God, so they could minister out of the relationship they had with Him. Jesus also said they would receive the Holy Spirit so that He could continue their training and teach them what they needed to know, so they could live this life they had been called to. We believe this is God's intention for the entire body of Christ.

Have you ever wanted to sit down with Jesus and ask Him questions about your life? Have you ever wished you could see life from God's perspective instead of your own? In order to develop a personal relationship with God and to live as God meant for us to live, we need to be able to have conversations with Him about our life. This means learning how to engage with the Spirit of God directly and listen to His voice. Once we learn how to engage with God in this manner, there are two amazing things that become available to us.

First, we get to be mentored directly by the Holy Spirit! A careful reading of John 14-17 shows us that when Jesus finished His ministry here on earth, He had not yet completed training His disciples. This was one of the main reasons He sent the Holy Spirit – so that everyone who came to faith could be mentored in the ways of the Kingdom by God Himself! In terms of our metaphor of rowing and sailing, learning how to be mentored by God is like learning to align the sail. Things can then happen in our life which we could never accomplish by "rowing" our way to change.

The second main benefit of learning how to make sense of God's revelations to us is that His voice carries with it the very power of life. When He speaks into our heart and mind, His words become food for our soul. He can also bring about healing and restoration we could experience no other way.

Learning how God speaks to us takes practice and guidance, just like learning a new language or learning how to sail. Our hope is that the practical approach in this session and the next will give you a good start (or refresher) on building your conversational prayer life with God.

---

3   Sessions 3 and 4 on Conversational Prayer are based on *Whispers of my Abba,* by David Takle

Notes **[Video: Session 3 – Part 1]**

What If ...
- We could be mentored by God in regard to our own life?
- The Holy Spirit could teach us the Bible and make it come alive for us?

What if we could have the kind of connection with God we read about in the Bible?

God Speaks!
- Some people have trouble believing God speaks in ways we can hear.
- The Bible is mostly about people who did or did not engage with God and what the resulting impact was on their lives.
- God is Relational! He wants to teach us how to live.

Conversational Prayer
- Many forms of prayer, each with a purpose:
  – Petition / praise / confession-repentance / intercession.
- Purpose of conversational prayer:
  – Communion with God is a <u>feast</u> for the soul (Isa.55).
  – Scripture comes alive.
  – We get to know God in relationship.
  – We see life more the way God sees it (through "the eyes of heaven").

  "With the eyes of your heart enlightened, you may know ..." (Eph.1:18).

Conversational Prayer
Four Aspects: Focusing, Listening, Discerning, Responding.

Quieting and Focusing
Come to God in faith and anticipation (Heb.11:6, next page).
In order to hear God we need to focus on Him and reduce the "static."
God does not usually talk over our noise level.
- Quiet my mind and let go of stress.
- Ask God to open my heart and mind to what He has for me.
- Ask God to reveal Himself to me.
  – Not a spectacular event, but an increasing awareness of Him.
- Look for Him with my heart (seeking, curious, longing, inquiring).
  – We are not passive in this process.

Help with Quieting
- Practical steps (remove distractions, have extra paper for notes).
- Physically relax: take deep breaths, yawn, stretch (to reduce tension).
- Listen to music.
  – Elisha used music to calm himself and help him focus (2Kg.3:15).
- Alternative: Pacing instead of sitting may help drain off nervous energy.

God Speaks!

(Ps.29) The voice of the Lord is powerful ... full of majesty ... it breaks the cedars ... it flashes forth flames of fire .. it causes the oaks to whirl ...

(Isa.55) Listen carefully to me, and eat what is good ... Incline your ear ... listen, so that you may live ... so shall my word be that goes out from my mouth; it shall not return to me empty, but it shall accomplish that which I purpose ...

(Mt.4:4) One does not live by bread alone, but by every word that comes from the mouth of God.

(Jn.5:25) I tell you, the hour is coming, and is now here, when the dead will hear the voice of the Son of God, and those who hear will live.

(Jn.6:45) It is written in the prophets, 'And they shall all be taught by God.' Everyone who has heard and learned from the Father comes to me.

(Jn.6:63) The words I have spoken to you are spirit and life.

(Jn.10:3,4,27) The sheep hear his voice. He calls his own sheep by name and leads them out ... the sheep follow him because they know his voice ... My sheep hear my voice. I know them and they follow me.

(Jn.14:26) But the Advocate, the Holy Spirit, whom the Father will send in my name, will teach you everything, and remind you of all that I have said to you.

(Jn.16:12-14) I still have many things to say to you, but you cannot bear them now. When the Spirit of truth comes, He will guide you into all the truth; for He will not speak on His own, but will speak whatever He hears, and He will declare to you the things that are to come. He will glorify me, because He will take what is mine and declare it to you.

(Rev.3:20,22) Listen! I am standing at the door, knocking; if you hear my voice and open the door, I will come in to you and eat with you, and you with me ... Let anyone who has an ear listen to what the Spirit is saying to the churches.

(Jn.5:39-40) You search the Scriptures, because you think that *in them* you have eternal life; and it is these that *bear witness of Me*; and you are unwilling to *come to Me*, that you may have life (emphasis added). (The purpose of Scripture is to point us to God for life.)

Our Part:
He who comes to God must believe that He is present, and that He responds to those who intentionally seek to engage with Him (Heb. 11:6, paraphrase).

Help with Focusing

"Fixing our eyes on Jesus, the author and finisher of our faith" (Heb.12:2)
which means using the eyes of our heart to focus on Him.

- Using the eyes of our heart.
  - Bible stories and Psalms stir up images in our mind.
  - Parables are word pictures of true things.
  - Biblical poetry uses rich imagery and metaphors to describe God and our life with Him.
- Recalling appreciation moments (see last session).
- Reading our previous journal entry.

The misuse of imagination does not prohibit its use any more than our ability to curse should keep us from talking.

Much of what God asks of us actually <u>requires</u> the use of imagination.

The Bible makes great use of metaphors and word pictures.

Exercise 3A – Quiet and Focus

Psalm 27 contains some very rich imagery that comes out of the writer's deep desire to be with God. He is probably out in the desert somewhere, imagining what it would be like to live in the Temple 24 hours a day, 7 days a week.

1. Allow yourself to relax. Recall an appreciation moment.
2. Invite God to reveal Himself to you and to open your heart to His presence.
3. Read the excerpt from Psalm 27 below.
   Try to join the Psalmist as he longs to be in the presence of God.
4. Record any pictures, impressions, emotions or words that come to mind.

"One thing I asked of the Lord, that will I seek after; to live in the house of the Lord all the days of my life; **to behold the beauty of the Lord**, and to inquire in his temple.... 'Come' my heart says, 'seek His face!' Your face, Lord, do I seek" (Ps.27:4,8).

[Video: Session 3 – Part 2]

Conversational Prayer – Listening
What is God's voice Like? How do we Listen?

God's Voice
- How does God speak to us?
  - Spirit to spirit

"The **Spirit** Himself testifies with our **spirit** that we are children of God" (Rom.8:16).

"This is what we speak, not in words taught us by human wisdom but in **words taught by the Spirit**, expressing spiritual truths **in spiritual words**. The man without the Spirit does not accept the things that come from the Spirit of God, for they are foolishness to him, and he cannot understand them, because they are *spiritually discerned* (1Cor.2:13-14).

- How do we experience Spirit-to-spirit communication?
  - Spontaneous words, thoughts, impressions, images.

Our Part in Listening
- <u>Reflecting</u>, by actively seeking, sensing, receiving, and being led.
  - Not passively waiting for something to surprise us.
  - Approaching in the demeanor of a student, always learning.
- <u>Noticing</u> internal reactions and responses.
  - Reveals what is in our heart and mind.
- <u>Verbalizing</u> our thoughts and impressions.
  - Writing or speaking out what comes to mind.
  - Words are important (this is *Conversational* prayer).
  - Gives substance to our impressions.
  - Helps us focus and use all our mind in the process.

Some other ways to describe listening:
- Can feel like being led through a fog.
- Often like searching for words to capture our impressions.

Conversation with God: Can also be described as <u>active spiritual reflection, with the expectation that God will speak to us</u>.

Listening to the Word
Allowing the Spirit of God to teach us about life in the Kingdom
     as He reveals the Word and our heart at the same time.
- Not settling for our own understanding of the text.
- Allowing the Spirit to reveal and internalize His truth.
- Focusing on short passages or phrases.

This approach to Scripture is not an attempt to master the text, or to figure out how to "apply" it, but a way of letting the Spirit reveal to us what we need to see and hear.

How to Listen to the Word
- Read the passage slowly, several times.
- Notice any reactions you have to a given word or phrase.
- Ask God to "unpack" each word or phrase and show you what you need.
- Receive, reflect, question, ponder, respond (flowing back and forth).

This is a way of engaging with the Spirit of God which Christians have used for centuries, allowing Him to minister the Word to our heart, making it come alive to where we are in our journey.

In this way, we actively participate with God to receive what He has for us.

Some great places to begin:

Isaiah 55 / Colossians 1,2,3 / Ephesians 1,2,3,4 / John 14,15,16,17

Psalms 23, 27, 84, 100, 139

(See a more complete description of Listening to the Word on page 44.)

The Importance of Conversational Prayer

It would be impossible to emphasize enough how important conversational prayer really is. If change comes from engaging with God, then nothing has the potential to change us more than being mentored by Him. Directly engaging with God can feed our soul, renew our mind, and transform our life.

So whatever difficulties you may experience, whatever resistance to regular practice you may feel, we strongly encourage you to persist and make this a priority in your life. *Nothing else will ever be as helpful* as learning how to engage with God and have conversations with Him.

This is one of the reasons why we ask you to seriously consider setting aside the time to practice this form of prayer on a regular basis for the duration of this course. The more you practice, and the more time you give to this, the more you will discover experientially how valuable it can be.

Important! Learning to have conversations with God may be ***the single most important thing*** you can do for your spiritual life.

Exercise 3B – Listening to God and the Word

Psalm 139 is a beautiful expression of the psalmist's trust that _God knows him and loves him completely at the same time_, and no matter where he goes or how far he strays he can never get lost.

(Please note: this Psalm has often been misunderstood as a fearful vision of God scrutinizing the psalmist, but it is actually a joyful expression of his total trust in God's goodness.)

1. Take a minute or two to quiet and focus. Recall an appreciation moment with God.
2. Ask God to show you His heart regarding the text below, and listen as you read.
3. Let some phrase or word capture your attention, allow it to fill your imagination, and ask God to reveal whatever He wants you to see in regard to that phrase.
4. Write down whatever feelings and impressions come to mind. (Use the space below and the next page.)

Do not try to cover the whole passage or worry too much about whether the words you write are your words or God's at this point. Simply begin your reflection with the anticipation that God is with you and will join you in this process.

Psalm 139

[1] O Lord, you have searched me and known me. [2] You know when I sit down and when I rise up; You discern my thoughts from far away. [3] You search out my path and my lying down, and are acquainted with all my ways. [4] Even before a word is on my tongue, O Lord, you know it completely. [5] You hem me in, behind and before, and lay your hand upon me.

[6] Such knowledge is too wonderful for me; it is so high that I cannot attain it.

[12] Even the darkness is not dark to you; the night is as bright as the day, for darkness is as light to you.

[13] For it was you who formed my inward parts; you knit me together in my mother's womb. [14] I praise you, for I am fearfully and wonderfully made; Wonderful are your works; that I know very well.

[23] Search me, O God, and know my heart; test me and know my thoughts. [24] See if there is any hurtful way in me, and lead me in the way everlasting.

Searched me and known me. I am as bright as day.

He has searched me and knows all my thoughts

(additional space for Exercise 3B)

Session 3 Sailing Practice – Reflecting On Abiding With God
JOHN 14-15

1. Be sure to continue the practice of turning your mind toward the goodness of God every morning and night for 5-10 minutes.

2. Read the article on *Listening to the Word* (next page).

3. Read the article on *Keeping a Prayer Journal* (page 46).

4. At this point, we would like to encourage you to begin a nine-week experiment in listening to the Word, using John's record of the "Upper Room Discourse" as a text. Please try to spend at least two times a week throughout the rest of this course during which you will reflect on the Gospel of John, chapters 14 and 15.

We highly recommend the following practice:
- Start a journal to keep a record of your reflections on these chapters.
- Begin each session asking God to open your heart to His teaching.
- Read your previous entry.
- If you feel led to move on, read only a few verses beyond where you read before.
- Use what you have learned about Listening to the Word to help you in your reflections.

There is no need to try and "make it through" the chapters by the end of the course. When it comes to this practice, depth is much better than distance. If you find yourself going over and over a particular word or phrase because it keeps yielding more fruit, then thank God for His ministry in your life and let Him show you what to do with this process. If you do find yourself at the end of chapter 15, then go back to chapter 14 and ask God to open your heart to even deeper things than you saw the first time through.

These chapters are some of the most beautiful revelations we have about God's desire to dwell with us. If we want to learn what it means to have a relationship with God, there are few places we could go for a better description of what that might look like. Savor these chapters and go back to them often.

Additional Reading on Conversational Prayer
David Takle: *Whispers of My Abba* (Shepherd's House: Pasadena) 2011
Dallas Willard: *Hearing God: Developing a Conversational Relationship with God* (IVP Books: Downers Grove, IL) 1999

The Practice of Listening to the Word

In our modern world, we talk fast, travel fast, and even pray fast. Our impatience to get to the end and our focus on completion rather than process are a real danger in reading Scripture, when every word is from God and has a power all its own. A lot can happen if we simply slow down and allow the Holy Spirit to speak to us about the words on the page and connect them to our journey at this particular place and time in our life.

Listening to the Word is reading for formation more than for information. We engage the text with the intention of being formed by it and to deepen our relationship with God. In this process we are making ourselves available to God, positioning ourselves before Him so that He might have access to our life.

The Process (source unknown)

1. Prayer of Preparation

   Yield all your cares and concerns to the Lord. Quiet your heart. Invite the Holy Spirit, who inspired the Word, to illumine its message to your heart.

2. Reading / Observation

   a)   Choose your text.
   b)   Read through the text slowly and thoughtfully.
   c)   Read through the text again, but this time read it out loud.
   d)   As you are reading, do so with the intent of hearing God's personal communication to you in and through the text.
   e)   Perhaps God will highlight a single word, phrase, or concept for you from the passage.
   f)   Do not stress out about this! It is not up to you to get God to speak to you. He is more than able to do so. All we are doing is putting ourselves in the position for Him to speak to us and engaging in the process.

3. Reflection / Pondering / Attraction

   a)   Take the word, phrase, or concept that God has spoken to you. Slowly turn it over in your mind. Allow it to interact with your inner world of concerns, memories, and ideas.
   b)   As you reflect, perhaps there are memories or images that surface.
   c)   Be aware of any emotions that surface in you, such as anxiety, peace, hope, frustration.
   d)   Listen to, ponder, and savor these words from God until they settle in your soul.
   e)   Remember, you are not alone in this process. God is with you. Allow Him to guide and direct you.

4. Response / Prayer / Dialogue with God

    a)   God is the one who has invited us into His loving embrace and this encounter with Him.

    b)   Interact with God as you would with one whom you know loves and accepts you.

    c)   Talk to God about what you have noticed. Tell Him about what has emerged for you so far in the process.

    d)   Ask God about things you do not understand.

    e)   Then, in silence, listen for what God seems to be communicating to you.

5. Contemplation / Rest

    a)   Allow yourself to let go of whatever is happening in your prayer in order to rest quietly in the presence and embrace of the God who loves you.

    b)   Simply rest in the Word of God and God's presence.

    c)   Simply be with God, resting in the unique one of a kind, unconditional love that God has for you.

Keeping a Prayer Journal

We strongly encourage you to try keeping a prayer journal, even if you have tried in the past without much success. It is very important to verbalize our conversations with God for the sake of focus, engaging our whole mind, and anchoring the words in reality. If possible, try journaling daily for the next two or three weeks.

How to Keep a Journal
- Date each entry.
- At the beginning of your conversation time, read your prior entry ("Remember").
- Discern whether to talk more about your prior topic (go deeper, try another angle) or start something new.
- If going on to another area, discern whether to discuss a life matter or Scripture phrase.
- Write out impressions, thoughts, questions, reactions, feelings, discernment, prayers.
- You can use full sentences or notes, but be sure to include enough to be able to make sense of what you have written. Sometimes short notes can become meaningless over time.
- Search for words that capture your impressions well.
- Keep an index page in the front or back of the journal, where you can identify key insights and healing moments so you can find them again easily.
- Reserve a few pages for ongoing prayer requests and to keep track of any discussions you might want to have with God in the future.

The Value of a Prayer Journal
- Helps us to jump start our conversations by reading prior entries.
- Provides continuity to our conversations from day to day.
- Helps us stay focused while we are talking to God.
- We do not lose our prior conversations over time.
- During a given conversation, we can scan what we have already written to restart our thoughts and provide additional promptings.
- Discernment is better when the material is in front of us.
- Keeps us actively involved; we are less likely to become too passive while listening.

Is it All Right for Christians to Visualize God ?

One of the more curious beliefs permeating much of Western Christianity is the idea that it is wrong to picture God in our mind. Evangelical leaders of considerable reputation have weighed in on this issue and expressed significant reservations about using our imagination to help us connect with God and experience His work in our life. "Heresy hunters" on the web would have you believe this is a deceptive New Age practice which is a direct violation of the second commandment, and that God will judge those who try to seek Him with this part of their mind.

Aside from the fact that the Mosaic Law only referred to making and worshiping <u>physical</u> images, this well-intentioned but misguided attempt to protect us is actually quite at odds with the rest of the Biblical record! Even a cursory glance through the Psalms should provide enough convincing evidence that <u>*the ancient Hebrews loved to imagine God*</u> in all sorts of ways. They wrote songs about Him, sang these songs directly to Him, and made sure the songs were recorded for all to see, so those who came after them could be taught this wonderful way of engaging with their Creator. Listen to a few of these phrases from the Psalms:

> "As for me, I shall behold your face in righteousness; when I awake I shall be satisfied, beholding your likeness" (17:15).

> "The Lord is my shepherd...he makes me lie down...you prepare a table before me...you anoint my head with oil" (23:1-5).

> "One thing I have asked...to behold the beauty of the Lord" (27:4).

> "The voice of the Lord breaks the cedars...shakes the wilderness...causes the oaks to whirl" (29:5-9).

> "He will cover you with his pinions, and under his wings you will find refuge" (91:4).

> "You are clothed with honor and majesty, wrapped in light as with a garment...you set the beams of your chambers on the waters, you make the clouds your chariot" (104:1-3).

These pictures are absolutely astounding. If they had been written by anyone today, they would very likely have been denounced by some people as "engaging in fantasy" or some other terrible practice. But these are not the ravings of a New Age cultist. They are writers inspired by God, describing their impressions of God, in ways that were sanctioned by God. If these had been violations of the second commandment, we would not have them in the Bible. If we were to go on and list all of the places where the psalmists and prophets used anthropomorphic language to describe God, it would take many pages. Clearly, the biblical authors believed in using their imaginations very freely as they thought about God.

What's more, Jesus Himself encouraged the use of imagination over and over in His ministry, when He used word pictures to describe the unseen realities of the Kingdom to those around Him. We call these parables. In many of them He painted for us some element of His Father's character. If using our imagination is such a dangerous practice, why would Jesus have persistently employed it in His teaching? Quite honestly, the biblical evidence is so heavily one-sided it's hard to imagine (irony intended) how this fear of our mental abilities has received such a large following.

While there is certainly such a thing as a *misuse* of the mind, we need to be careful not to "throw the baby out with the bathwater." If we stop and think about it, turning off our imagination is actually quite difficult, if not impossible. You may have just imagined a baby being poured out with the water from a small tub! Or you may have pictured what it would be like to turn off your imagination with a switch.

The truth is *God deliberately created our minds with the ability to "see" things that are not in our immediate field of vision.* Our imaginative capacity allows us to picture better ways of doing things, it allows us to rehearse possible outcomes before attempting something difficult, and it allows us to transmit meaning with stories and metaphors that are far more potent than descriptive prose can ever be. This is one of the reasons why Jesus used word pictures all the time in His teaching.

Bible stories often stir up our imagination and give us a chance to compare our own responses to those of the characters in the text. For example, it is one thing to be told God forgives us unconditionally and quite another to run a video in our mind of the parable of the Prodigal. The image of the Father running out to meet his long-lost son can communicate very powerful meanings to us that penetrate far more deeply than any forensic description of forgiveness. Stories are so important that many times in both the Old and New Testaments we are told to *remember* the things God has done for us (that is, tell the story again in your community). In this sense we are *commanded* to use our imaginations.

The ability to *misuse* imagination does not prohibit our use of it any more than our ability to curse should prohibit us from talking. Aside from the fact that we probably would have to be in denial in order to think we are *not* using our imagination, abandoning our ability to picture holy things would actually make parables incomprehensible, put much of our mind out of reach of God's redemption, and violate the command to love God "with all your mind." How does one think about whatever is "lovely, pure, true, just, honorable, or commendable" (Phil.4:8) without imagining how those things might look in the real world? How do you "remember the Lord's death" without seeing Him on the cross? How do we "fix our eyes on Jesus" (Heb.12:2) when He is no longer here in the flesh?

We could go on. Story telling has been used from the beginning of time to teach important principles to children so they can learn from the experiences of others without having to make all the mistakes themselves. This is most certainly a use of our mind intended by God.

When we read that the psalmist longed to "behold the beauty of the Lord" (Ps.27:4), what are we supposed to think went through his mind, given that he could never really *see* God? When Jesus told the disciples the Holy Spirit would become their new teacher, did He not intend for them to think about how <u>He</u> had been their teacher, and how those conversations would be both similar to and different from the way He had taught them? When the first generation of disciples broke bread together in remembrance of Christ, did not images of Jesus necessarily come to mind? Was it wrong? Is it now wrong for us to imagine Him breaking bread because we never saw Him in the flesh?

The fear of using our imaginations really makes very little sense. Consider the value of seeing God's gift to us as a "treasure in earthen vessels" (2Cor.4:7), or envisioning ourselves as clay in the potter's hands (Isa.64:8). Imagination is a <u>*good*</u> thing, because it helps us know who we are, where we have come from, and who this God is who cares so much about us. It is a <u>*good*</u> thing to imagine ourselves having a conversation with God, to imagine His very presence with us, and to imagine His involvement in our life.

So what is the basic difference between holy imagination and New Age fantasy? **In a word – holy imagination actually brings us <u>*closer*</u> to reality. New Age fantasy moves us <u>*away*</u> from reality.**

This is not something to be afraid of – it is something we can embrace with a passion. When we begin to fill our mind with thoughts of God and seek to connect with Him deeply, we put great distance between us and any cult practice where people try to connect with whatever happens to be flying through the cosmos. All we really need to do is ask God to guard our heart and mind, and trust Him to meet us in the process. We can ask Him to give us a revelation of His presence, a meaningful image of His relationship to us, or a picture that we need for comfort. And even as Jesus used pictures which were highly relevant to the farmers and peasants who listened to His words, God will give us images and impressions that have substance and meaning for us.

This bears repeating. God gave us the ability to picture things in our mind that are not within our immediate field of vision. Not only is this helpful in the physical world – so that we have the sense to look under the bed for the clothes we wore yesterday – it also helps us to see the unseen Kingdom of God we have been invited to live in, because it is not something we can behold with our physical eyes.

So when the writer of Hebrews talks about "fixing our eyes on Jesus," he is referring to the eyes of our heart, that is, our ability to focus our mind in a way that allows us to see this amazing God we get to be with. God created us with this ability, He evoked its use when He walked among us, and His people have made tremendous use of it for centuries in their writings. The enemy of our souls could never have given us this. It was entirely God's idea to help us engage with Him more deeply. The only thing the enemy could do was make up some ways of misusing it.

Those who came up with this fear of imagination did not get it from Scripture. Perhaps they opted for turning off the whole mental process as much as possible in an effort to be "safe." While it is true that we may need help with learning how to use our imagination in holy ways, we do not need to fear imagination itself or create theologies out of thin air in order to avoid getting the help we need.

The only caution we might add for those who have had extensive experience in the occult in the past is that this may be a bit more complex. Anyone who has a history of direct contact with demonic forces may need special help sorting things out in their mind and prayer life. They should seek out Christians who know Scripture well and have some experience with discerning what is really God and what is a counterfeit.

The presence of God is an awesome thing. The ways He wants to work in us and with us go way beyond whatever we could figure out from a purely logical application of the principles we can find in Scripture. In order to have an authentic, substantive relationship with God, we need to learn how to see Him, sense His presence with us, and envision His work in us. And God has every intention of employing our ability *to see the unseen* as part of this process.

May God give you freedom and joy as He makes use of your holy imagination to help you to experience Him more fully!

Ship's Log – Session 3

I am remembering today how I used to have a kind of love-hate experience in regard to reading the Bible. I knew it was *supposed* to be important – I even taught a class once on how much we needed to read the Bible. But the truth was I would often go weeks at a time without picking one up. Sometimes I would have to dust it off before I opened it. Of course, I would feel ashamed of myself for having neglected the whole project, and tell myself over and over I needed to read it more. And for a time I would keep at it, only to drift away after a while, and then the whole cycle would repeat itself.

I never did understand why something so inherently valuable could be so dry and tasteless so much of the time. Honestly, reading the Bible usually felt more like doing homework than feeding my soul. What's more, the harder I tried to make it interesting, the more it felt like work. Sometimes I wondered if it was *supposed* to be hard, so that we would have to be really *committed* in order to make it "work" for us. Maybe God was testing our commitment level more than our reading comprehension after all.

Then I heard about how to listen to the Word and how to be taught by the Spirit of God instead of trying to analyze the text on my own. The difference was amazing! What life! What food for my soul! Words came alive and jumped off the page and penetrated my heart! Passages I had read a hundred times before rang true in my soul as if I had never heard them before.

I finally understood what Jesus meant when He said, "You diligently scour the scriptures, because you think you will find life in between the letters of the text. But you are missing the point. The purpose of the scriptures is to point you back to me, so that you would come to me, and in so doing you would find life!" (paraphrased). He was describing my very own experience! I had combed the pages of the Bible for years and come up empty. But when I came to Him and asked Him what He wanted to show me, using a word or phrase from the Bible as a springboard for our conversation, I found life! He showed me His heart, His goodness, His care for my soul. He gently exposed places in me I knew very little about, which needed His kind, mentoring words to heal and restore. He showed me things about Kingdom Life and spoke them into my heart and soul in ways I could never have internalized on my own.

Most of all, I could not wait to spend time with Him to see what He had in store for me each day. Since then, His love for me has become more real, more tangible than I ever thought possible. As time goes on I find I am becoming more and more dependent on what He feeds me with, so when I miss a day or two I often feel as if I'm languishing, starving for what He alone can give me.

Now I do not mean to imply that every day brings about wholesale transformation. While there truly are moments when His insights are so beautiful that it is as if someone turned on a light in the room, most of the time it is more like a cool drink of water, a life-giving hug from God, or a breath of fresh air. Sometimes we sit quietly together, so I can simply enjoy His presence around me, enfolding me in His love. And yes, I do have seasons from time to time where seeing Him is difficult and hearing Him is hard. I feel homesick and separated from my life. As in any other relationship, my heart has its own reasons for holding back or running away. But when I stop running and seek Him out, He is always closer than I imagined.

David Takle
Sailor Apprentice

SESSION 4 – DEVELOPING A CONVERSATIONAL PRAYER LIFE (PART 2)
DISCERNING AND RESPONDING

One of the reasons many people shy away from conversational prayer is the problem of knowing the difference between hearing something from God and making things up! How do you tell when your spontaneous thoughts are coming from God and when they are your own impulsive thoughts? How can you have any faith in what you are hearing if you are not sure of the source? Is there any danger in hearing something from the enemy of our souls?

In this session we will talk about discerning, which involves much more than identifying God's voice. As we will see, discerning is primarily an act of *noticing or observing*. An important part of maturity is the ability to see *how we ourselves are involved* in whatever is going on around us. In the case of conversational prayer, we must be mindful at all times, no matter how much we feel carried along by the process, that we are intimately involved at all levels of the interaction. For example, our trust level influences the quality of our connection, our presuppositions can distort what we "hear," and the choices we make each step of the way determine whether we become more or less engaged in what God has for us.

So for our time with God to be fruitful, we not only need to pay attention to what God is saying, we need to *pay attention to how well we are paying attention*. We need to notice when something we think we heard runs contrary to the character of God. If we have been sitting quietly for several minutes with no thoughts of anything at all, we need to notice and ask God what to do in order to get back on track. If we have a negative reaction to a verse of Scripture or feel resistance to some area we think needs attention, then we need to tell God what we are feeling and look to Him for the next step in our process.

Thus, discernment is almost like having another pair of eyes present, observing our interaction with God and willing to be honest about what we see, both in terms of what is life-giving and what is not. In some ways, this is similar to how we engage in conversation with people we care about. We pay attention to their tone, their inflections, the way they phrase their sentences, and even what we think is being left unsaid. All of these factors go into how we make sense of what they are saying to us. In a word, this is practicing discernment in our everyday conversations. Our conversations with God may involve some different dynamics, but we still try to pay attention on several levels at once.

We are also going to talk about responding, which is about what we do with what we receive during our conversations. Our focus here will be on some ways in which we can more deeply internalize and retain what we receive during our times with God. Spending focused time with God is life-giving in and of itself, and receiving life from God is reason enough to engage with Him. However, throughout our time of conversational prayer, there are usually many opportunities to draw us deeper into our connection with God, as well as ways that we can participate more actively in the process of internalizing truth. And as our focused times draw to a close, it is important to discern ways in which we can help to hold on to what we have been given.

Exercise 4A – Remember Psalm 139

One of the best ways to connect with God is to recall a previous conversation we had with Him or a previous time of reflection.

"I will call to mind the deeds of the Lord ... I will meditate on all your works" (Ps.77:11-12 NRSV).

1. Spend a few minutes quieting and remembering your previous reflection on Psalm 139 (Exercise 3B). If God gave you some life-giving perspective during that exercise, re-read your notes and recall what He revealed to you.
2. Read the excerpt from Psalm 139 below, taken from the New Living Translation. Reading from a different translation often helps to foster new ways of seeing the passage.
3. Consider what it means to be totally known and loved at the same time.
4. Write out your heart's response.

"O Lord, you have examined my heart and know everything about me...You chart the path ahead of me and tell me where to stop and rest...You both precede and follow me. You place your hand of blessing on my head. Such knowledge is too wonderful for me, too great for me to know!" (NLT).

[Video: Session 4 – Part 1]

Conversational Prayer
Focus, Listen, Discern, Respond.

Discerning
There are two major areas requiring discernment.
- <u>Process</u> – **how** the conversation is proceeding.
- <u>Content</u> – **what** is coming to mind.

Discerning the Process
Making observations about **what we are presently doing.**
- Am I quiet / focused / on track?
- Listening well or over-analyzing?
- Do these words capture my impressions?
- We need to ask these kinds of questions because we can …
  - Get distracted / Drift off topic in our thinking.
  - Run out of steam or find ourselves in a place that is not fruitful.
  - Trivialize important things or over-emphasize things that are not helpful.
  - Become too analytical and stop listening.

Discerning the Process
- Paying attention to **where we need to go from here.**
- Experiencing any of these inclinations may be clues about where to proceed.
  - Urging / Longing – noticing the stirring of our true heart's desires.
  - Attention / Curiosity – maintaining the mind of a lifelong learner.
  - Doubt / Disbelief – noticing gaps in our trust and in our development.
- Maintaining an expectation to be led in the process.
  - Am I still missing something? What else do I need to see?

Discerning the Content
When it comes to discerning the thoughts that come to mind, there is a
major difference between discernment and censorship.

- <u>Discernment</u>
Needs to be trusting, graceful, honest, non-condemning.
  - An *observation* about the quality of the content without condemnation.
  - A *decision* about what to do with the observations.
  - **Goal:** to remain teachable and relational – to keep learning.
Remaining teachable means everything I write down is subject to revision.
Staying relational means relying on the Spirit to assist my judgment.
  - I am a continual learner, not a perfectionist.
  - My main job is to learn how to learn from God.

- Censorship
  - Fear based – afraid of getting something wrong or unbiblical.
  - Prevents thoughts from taking shape.
  - **Goal:** To avoid mistakes – to manage the conversation.
    Includes trying to come up with the "right" answers instead of being honest about our thoughts, attitudes, feelings.

Notice the difference in goals. If Peter had held on to avoiding mistakes, he might not have gone to preach to Cornelius. By remaining teachable, he stepped out of his prior assumptions and made the leap to acknowledging that Gentiles could receive the Holy Spirit.

Please read the article, *What If I Hear Something Wrong,* at the end of the Session.

Discerning the Content

What sort of **content** can we expect God to reveal?

The "Eyes of Heaven" to see God, self, and life the way God sees them.

- What we do not know about our own heart (may be confrontational).
- Significance of things we thought we knew (new depth perception).
  Often happens through asking new questions.
- Reminders of things easily forgotten (Jn.14:26).
- Healing words – Truth that re-frames our story.
  How God tells us our story is different than how we have understood our own story. God's version is redemptive.
- His heart for us, how much He loves us.

How Do I Know if it's God?

- God's word to us has the power of life in it.
- The more life-giving quality there is to the content, the more we can be sure it comes from God – His thoughts are different and better.
- Bears fruit.
  - Immediate: resolution, peace, love, excitement, awe.
    Seeing something important with far more clarity.
  - Long term: attitudes and expectations are more God-centered.
- God's confrontations are gentle and caring.
  - Harsh condemnation is from our own background or from the Accuser.
- Check with your community (assuming that it's healthy!) for confirmation.
- We learn from experience.
  - As we become more familiar with God's heart through our own experience and through the ways His heart is revealed in Scripture, we recognize it better.

Experience is our primary means of learning discernment. This is one reason why we need to spend a lot of time with God. (But we need to remain teachable in this area, knowing that we may need help understanding our spiritual experiences.)

Exercise 4B – Discussing an Important Issue With God

In the previous session, we spent some time in conversation with the Spirit of God, asking Him to open our eyes to whatever He wanted to show us regarding Psalm 139. Using Scripture is a great way for us to begin a conversation with God. But we can also use a life issue as the starting point for our conversation.

1. Take a few moments to quiet and focus. Rest as much as possible in the presence of God. Recall an appreciation moment.

2. Ask God one of the following questions:

    (a) God, how do You see our relationship?

    If this question raises a lot of anxiety or defensiveness in you, or if nothing at all comes to mind, then consider this question instead:

    (b) God, what do I need to know about You that would make the first question more addressable?

    or possibly:

    (c) God, what can you tell me about the fear and defensiveness I feel when I think about asking you how You see our relationship?

3. Write out whatever feelings come up and whatever you sense God may be saying to you. (Don't try to guess what He would say, let it come to you.) Write as you feel led, and when the stream slows down, ask God to draw you to whatever it is He wants you to really focus on.

    If nothing comes to mind, begin by telling God how the relationship looks from your point of view. After sharing your perspective for a few minutes, ask Him if He sees it any differently.

    If your conversation slows down but does not feel resolved, go back to exercise 3B and ask God how Psalm 139 can help you see more of how He cares about you.

(this page is for use with Exercise 4B)

[Video: Session 4 – Part 2]

Conversational Prayer – Responding
- Why we need to respond actively.
- Where do I need to focus my attention?
  - Depth generates more growth than breadth.
- How do I make this "stick"?

Responding – Questions That May Help
- God, what do you want me to hold on to from our time together?
- How can I act on this?
- What do I want to come back to again?

Ways to Respond
- Quiet-together time with God.
- Enjoying the moment – reflecting and letting things sink in for a while.
- Prayers we may be led to (possibly writing them out):
  - Thanksgiving / Praise / Intercession
  - Repentance / Renunciation
- Actions we can take:
  - Contact / Connect
  - Forgiveness / Amends
  - Serve / Give
  - Memorize Verse(s) – review several times a day
  - Post a note to keep the thought visible
  - Share with others

Long Term Impact of Conversational Prayer
- Process becomes more fluid.
  - Focus / Listen / Discern / Respond.
- Deeper relationship with God.
  - Experiential relationship, not limited to ideas *about* God.
  - Get to know His character.
  - How He loves and cares for me.
  - How He speaks to me.
- Healing and transformation.
  - Mentoring relationship brings growth, healing, victory.

Conversational Prayer
- Communion with God is a <u>feast</u>!
- Reflecting with anticipation is the primary bridge to conversations.
  - Focus / Listen / Discern / Respond.

Session 4 Sailing Practice – Ongoing

1. Focus on the goodness of God each morning and night (Appreciating the Goodness of God).
2. Listen to the Spirit teach you about abiding in John 14-15 (Directly Interacting).

Session 4 Sailing Practice – Reflecting on a Snapshot of Life

(Adapted from: Dallas Willard and Jan Johnson:
    Renovation of the Heart in Daily Practice, NavPress 2006, p.143, used by permission)

Choose an image from the Psalms below that best describes your soul and the things it wants to cry out. If you can't decide, choose the one your best friend or spouse would choose for you.

A panting deer who has been running in search of water for a long time (42:1).
A small creature crouching in the protective shadow of a huge creature (God's wings) (57:1).
A weary desert traveler (63:1).
An ailing patient who stretches out his hands for help, yet refuses to be comforted
        when comfort is offered (77:2).
Someone who has narrowly escaped death (116:8).
A tired mountain climber who has found a solid foothold (94:18-19).
A gourmet dinner (63:5) (or Isa.55:1-3).

Consider the image you've chosen. What is the cry of your soul based on that image? What is needed to help your soul rest in God?

Additional Reading on Conversational Prayer

David Takle: *Whispers of My Abba* (Shepherd's House: Pasadena) 2011
Dallas Willard: *Hearing God: Developing a Conversational Relationship with God* (IVP Books: Downers Grove, IL) 1999

What If I Hear Something Wrong?

One of the most common issues people have in regard to hearing God is the fear of hearing something from the enemy, or the related fear of mistaking our own thoughts for a word from God. Certainly we do not want to be led astray, so this fear is not completely unfounded. However, this fear is terribly misplaced. For the most part, we really do not need to be afraid of hearing something wrong, and there are several reasons why this is true.

First, we need to understand clearly that our minds are full of faulty ideas already. These faulty ideas are in fact driving our lives and affecting us tremendously in very negative ways. So to be afraid of having an incorrect thought and mistaking it for something from God is a bit like being afraid of getting dirty while cleaning out the garage. It is going to happen. There is no reason why the things we hear during our conversations with God should be infallible or why we should always be able to correctly identify their source. We are perhaps more like Peter than we think.

Second, much of what God does when He speaks with us is to reveal our faulty thinking and show us better ways to understand life in the Kingdom. We see this often in the ministry of Jesus as He trained His disciples. If the Holy Spirit's job is to renew our minds and heal the distorted ideas of life that we already have, then we can be sure He is able to help us when we get confused about what is from God and what is not from God while talking to Him. This is simply part of what He does anyway.

The key to hearing well and noticing when we need to revisit something we thought we heard, is to remain always the student, always teachable, and always open to new understanding about things we think we already know. We can check out ideas out with God, we can wait a few weeks and ask again, and we can ask someone who is farther along to help us when we are unsure of what to do with something. As long as we are willing to revise our understanding, we need not be too afraid of hearing what God has to say about our life and trusting Him to help us discern the truth of what we hear.

The problem comes in when we feel the need to defend our interpretations about what we hear. Sometimes people get the mistaken idea that their own credibility or self-worth is on the line if they have to retract or revise something they thought was from God. Once we accept that we are still learning how to learn, and may continue to do so for the rest of our lives, we are more able to let go of any felt need to be right. This is not a test, but a relationship with a God who is infinitely patient with our attempts to learn. We need to give ourselves the space and grace to make mistakes.

Another problem which can get in the way of remaining teachable is our potential disappointment over having thought we heard something right, then needing to admit to ourselves at a later time that it probably was not God after all. We may feel like we can no longer trust our ability to tell what is God and what is not. This kind of disappointment can be serious, because we might give up on trying to hear anything at all. But what we really need is to take the issue back to God and tell Him we need more help in this area than we thought, and ask Him to mentor us more in how to discern. And perhaps ask Him to send us someone who can help us with this as well.

A Model for Conversational Prayer (Summary)

The Holy Spirit loves to teach! One of His most important ministries is to be your personal Mentor in regard to life. He especially wants to teach you in regard to your own heart and the things that get in the way of living life the way God intended: distorted images of yourself, distorted images of who God is, distorted ideas of how life works in the Kingdom, and confusion about love and relationships. Like any good mentor, He wants to engage with you in the process of discovery, not hand you black and white answers. So "listening" can be a very interactive process. As the Spirit of Truth, He can speak truth that is transformational, most notably during "teachable moments" of life. Examples of teachable moments are:

- when emotions run high.
- during periods of intense confusion.
- when you set aside time for the purpose of engaging with Him.

The following model offers a simple means of engaging in dialogue with God that most people find quite helpful. Remember that listening to God and having two-way conversations with Him is a learned process that will grow with time, and is impacted by a variety of maturity factors. Allow yourself the grace to be uncertain at times, and to acknowledge when listening to God seems difficult.

Hearing God involves all four of the facets discussed on the following pages. While we must almost always begin with quieting and focusing, the process of engaging with God involves all four areas, flowing back and forth in a rather fluid motion. As you learn to pay attention to what is going on while you are listening to God, you may find yourself drawn more toward one area at any given moment. It is usually important to follow this leading rather than attempt to hold to any rigid format.

A great way to begin this process is to ask God to open the Word to you as you read (much like the psalmist does in Ps.119:18). A good place to start is with one of the following passages, because they are very rich in what they say about who we are in God's eyes and what He has given to us for life.

Isaiah 55, Psalms 23, 27, 84, 100, and 139, John 14-17, Ephesians 1-4, and Colossians 1-3.

1. Quieting and Focusing

The goal here is to quiet your mind and seek to be aware of God's presence. This is not a New Age exercise of emptying your mind completely or opening up to "whatever is out there," but a way of allowing God to fill your mind with *His* presence, and reducing the amount of "static" that keeps you from hearing your deepest thoughts. For those who can get to a place of rest easily, simply quiet down, take a few deep breaths, and let go of all distractions. For those who have difficulty with this, try walking around in a relatively peaceful area where there are no distractions. This can help drain off the excess energy so you can focus better.

Pray a short prayer for God to reveal Himself to you, and accept by faith that you are in the presence of the Holy Spirit and will be guided by Him. Ask Jesus to help you see Him and focus the eyes of your heart on Him.

2. Listening

God's voice most often comes to us in the form of spontaneous thoughts rather than in audible words. Be prepared to pay attention to your body, your emotional reactions, the Spirit of God, and your spontaneous thoughts. This is mostly about receiving or being led through a process, not over-analyzing a text or relying on your own ability to find applications. Begin your discussion with God, and ask Him about a word or phrase you have read in Scripture that caught your attention, or ask Him any question for which you would like His mentoring and teaching (not a yes/no question). For example, "God, what do I need to know today about my relationship to You?"

Either write out (if sitting) or carry on the conversation vocally (if pacing), writing or speaking whatever comes to you. Include your own thoughts and feel free to paraphrase any impressions that seem to originate from God. *The goal is not to be able to quote God but to engage with Him*. Feel free to ask further clarifying questions and to say what you currently believe about the issue at hand. Be honest about your reactions, and be open to spontaneous thoughts that address the issue differently from what you might have predicted or thought proper.

3. Discerning

Of course, not everything going through your mind originates with God. Be aware of when you are clearly working things through on your own (which is fine as long as you are aware of it). Allow the Spirit to prompt you when your thoughts stray too much, and be willing to question things after you have written them down. You can also go back to earlier points in your discussion to get back on track. Ask some of the questions again if necessary. The main point here is to remain teachable and open to revising your earlier thoughts. Truth sometimes emerges slowly, over time. Something that sounds good to us at one point may need to be further refined later on.

After the flow quiets down, go over your conversation and ask God to draw you to whatever it is He wants you to learn from this. It is not always necessary to identify who said what. Rather, tune in to whatever God wants you to take away from the conversation. Be open to asking a trusted friend or your community for help discerning whether or not what you received came from God.

4. Responding

You may feel led to pray a prayer of thanksgiving, of forgiveness, of repentance; or pray for strength, resolve, or encouragement; or take action in some area of your life. If you received some enlightening truth, consider writing it out somewhere to remind you in the coming days.

We hope this short description of conversational prayer has been helpful.

Ship's Log – Session 4

Engaging with God over life issues can be one of the most life-giving experiences we can have, as God shows us what we have missed and what we need in order to move on. But we need to stay teachable, because these issues often have more than one layer to them.

For example, during one conversation I had with God about my self-hate, He gave me an insight that healed my self-image in some very important ways. He revealed how many of the terrible things I believed about myself had more to do with the ways my family saw me during my early childhood than it had to do with who I really am in God's eyes. It was a life-giving moment, as if I had been given a cool drink of water in the desert.

But along with the healing, I uncovered a lot of buried anger about the injustice of having received such a destructive sense of self from my parents – a powerful hatred of myself which I had lived with for decades. It was only in a later conversation with God that He revealed to me how they had been as much if not more wounded than I was in this area and could not have possibly given me a sense of self they did not possess themselves. I had known this in theory, of course, but when God spoke it into my heart, it rang true. It was a correction I needed in regard to how my sense of self had been damaged. Although my prior conversation had given me an important truth, I had also internalized a faulty view of my parents that God needed to address.

When I sit down to spend time with God, sometimes I begin with a passage of Scripture, and other times I bring up whatever I am dealing with at the time. Either way, God reveals His heart to me and helps me see things from His perspective. Most encounters with Him are like meeting with the Father I always wished I had – who always has time for me, always knows what I need, and knows how I need to hear it so that I "get" it.

Over time this has become a way of living, a way of proceeding that has far more heart than I ever knew before, and more hope than I ever dreamed possible. More and more, I anticipate God's care for me as well as His particular lessons on life. I trust Him more, I love Him more, and I feel more secure in my journey with Him with each passing year.

The other day I ran across the verses in Romans 8 where Paul asks, "Who or what could possibly separate us from the love of God? Hardship? Distress? Hunger? Danger? (He has quite a list here, much of which he himself experienced.) He goes on to declare there is nothing that can separate us. So I started listing all the things in my life that have derailed me or come close to derailing me. It turns out I have quite a list, too. That's when I felt led to recall all the ways in which God has restored my life. Man, that was fun! What a long list of mentors, healings, great books, wonderful teachers and so on He has used to overcome all the things which might have otherwise separated me from God's love. It was great to spend time with God, rejoicing and thanking Him for all the ways He has shown His love to me. And that was just one day's re-alignment of the sail!

David Takle
Sailor Apprentice

SESSION 5 – GRACE AS A MEANS FOR TRANSFORMATION
GRACE IS AN AGENT FOR CHANGE

Next to love, *grace* is perhaps the most broadly applied term in the New Testament in regard to God's action in the lives of His people. Learning to live in grace is absolutely foundational to receiving life from God and being transformed into the people He created us to be.

Unfortunately, while most of us have learned to associate the term "grace" with what happens to us at the time of our conversion, relatively few Christians have a clear understanding of what grace has to do with *growing* as a Christian. We tend to think of conversion as God's job and the Christian life as our job. This is in fact a very weak understanding of both grace and the Christian life.

Understanding how grace works into the life of a Christian is critically important. Otherwise, we will not be able to balance our part and God's part when it comes to growing up spiritually. Many of us take on too much of the task and try to crank out our growth through a lot of "spiritual" activity. Others become too passive in regard to their spiritual development and expect God to ambush them or take over their will and make them do what they need to. Either way, assuming too much of the job or engaging the task too passively, we do not receive enough of what we need in order to be changed.

Learning how to <u>participate</u> with God is essential to receiving His work in our heart and mind. God has so much He wants to do in us to make us into the people He intends for us to be. But He can only change us as we engage with Him in ways that are in concert with the true nature of our relationship with Him. If we try to do His job or fail to do our part in this process, then it will not matter how dedicated we are to our approach – it simply will not bear the kind of fruit we desire.

Perhaps one of the best analogies for how grace works is that of the relationship between good parents and a young child. The parents have all the resources needed for the child's well-being, but the child needs to participate with his or her parents in every way. When hungry, the child has to come to Mom or Dad for food and eat what is set before him. When he scrapes his knee, he needs to allow his parent to cleanse and treat the wound. When sick, he needs to take the medicine Mom provides. When he breaks something, he needs to bring it to Dad to be repaired. There are also many ways that Mom and Dad model for the child how to engage with life and how to ask for help when he has difficulty. All of these things are examples of grace in the child's life. These are things small children cannot do for themselves, but in which they need to cooperate with Mom and Dad in order to receive what they need.

Furthermore, we need to point out how all of this happens *inter-personally*, between the parents and the child. In the same way, we need to engage with God on a very *personal* level for what we need. It is never enough to simply read the Bible like a technical manual and attempt to do what it says. In this session, we will describe God's grace from several angles that, hopefully, will provide a better sense of the ways in which spiritual growth is actually a work of grace in which we are active participants, and not a result of trying hard to be a good Christian.

Notes # Helps for those having difficulty with Conversational Prayer

Continue to Practice Spiritual Reflection

Spiritual Reflection is one of our best bridges to directly engaging with God.

- Written or spoken – be sure to put words to your reflective thoughts.
- Express your heart – longings, appreciation, doubt, fear, confusion.
- Think of reflection like sitting down with your mentor, who says, "Tell me what's on your heart."

  Your part is to reflectively go over what you know, what you want, and what you think you may be missing. Share all of that with Him and ask Him to help you discover what you are missing.

- Make good use of appreciation moments to increase your awareness of God.

Be Careful About Being Too Passive

- Hearing God is <u>not</u> done by making your mind go blank and waiting for something to jump into your head.
- Pausing momentarily to pay attention to promptings can be helpful, but that is not the same as emptying your mind and waiting.

Talk to God About Your Difficulty

- Seems redundant, but it helps many people.
- Tell Him what you want.
  - What you are currently experiencing.
  - What you feel in regard to this issue.
- Ask Him, "What am I missing? What do I need?"

Trust That ...

- He has put His Spirit in you and is truly present with you.
- He has breathed life into your spirit.
- He wants to reveal Himself to you.
- Your new heart naturally gravitates toward the things of God.
- You have the capacity to be curious about the things of God.
- You have the capacity to desire good things.

Remember:

Conversational prayer is primarily learned though <u>experience</u>. It is very important to set aside a regular time you can count on to engage with God, so you can develop your sensitivity to His presence and learn better how to interact with Him.

Exercise 5A – Quiet

It is easy to get caught up in the demands of the world around us and forget that we live in the presence of God. Allowing yourself to rest with God is a valuable way to remember who you are, whose you are and what is truly important.

Ask the Spirit of God to calm your body and soul and to open your heart to His presence.
Read the verses below and allow yourself to feel the peace of God.

> "He makes me lie down in green pastures; He leads me beside **quiet** waters" (Ps.23:2).

> "My soul, wait in **silence** for God only, For my hope is from Him" (Ps.62:5).

For the next few minutes simply rest in Him.

[Video: Session 5 – Part 1]

Grace as a Means for Transformation
- What is Grace?
- What does it have to do with forming Christian character?

Have You Heard These Statements?
- "Salvation is something *God* does out of His love for us,
    and the Christian Life is something *we* do for God out of our love for Him."
  - Assumes I can actually live the Christian life if I care enough and try hard.
    Although very common, this is a faulty assumption.
  - Reduces our relationship to a spiritual transaction.

- "If I try my best to live the Christian life,
    the Holy Spirit will give me the strength to do it."
  - Fails to explain burnout, bondage to sin, or wounds that do not heal.
  - Often we cannot tell where our effort leaves off and God's begins.
  - Assumes the starting point for interaction is self-effort.
  - Focuses on doing more rather than becoming more.

Grace (Common understanding)
Grace is about getting saved (having sins forgiven).
"I get something I don't deserve" (heaven).
"I don't get something I do deserve" (punishment).
These are very limited perceptions of Grace.

Grace (Properly understood)
Everything God does **for** us and **in** us
    that we cannot do for ourselves (Dallas Willard).

Both salvation and spiritual growth involve receiving from God what we cannot do
    for ourselves. We are no more capable of spiritual growth than we are of
    salvation.
Grace is not only something we need to <u>become</u> Christians.
We need it to <u>grow</u>. Grace is actually **a means for Change.**

  "Having started with the Spirit, are you now ending with the flesh?" (Gal.3:3).

  "Therefore as you have **received** Christ Jesus the Lord, so **walk** in Him" (Col.2:6).

We do <u>not</u> have two different spiritual laws at work, one by which to get saved and
    another by which to grow spiritually.
We cannot overcome evil by our own effort, any more than we can become a child
    of God by our own effort.
We *become* Christians by coming to God. We *grow* as Christians by coming to God.

What God Does For Us (that we cannot do)

- Enters into a living relationship with us.
- Gives us a new identity.
- Progressively heals us from the <u>effects</u> of sin committed *by* us
    (not only removing the guilt, but cleaning up the damage left behind).
- Progressively heals us from the <u>effects</u> of sin committed *against* us.
- Progressively removes in us the <u>causes</u> of sin.
- Changes our heart to be more like His.
- Mentors us in regard to our own life (renews our mind).

These are all <u>gifts</u> we cannot get any other way than to be given them by God. This is why it is so important to engage with God. Christian growth is not a reward for trying hard, it is a gift <u>received</u> from engaging with God (that's <u>grace</u>).

God has decided to bond with us, to live inside us, to heal and restore in us that which was damaged by this broken world. These are all acts of <u>grace</u> – amazing gifts of restoration from ruin, all beyond our ability to initiate or do.

Legalism as a Way of Life

Legalism is *not* about being more rule-oriented than someone else.

Legalism is both a belief and an action:

- **Belief:** Righteousness is <u>doing</u> what is right, and <u>not doing</u> what is wrong.
- **Action:** Attempting to become righteous by trying to live up to a high standard of behavior.

This has been a problem throughout the history of the church.

Jesus faced it with the Pharisees – Paul addressed it in Galatians and elsewhere.

TRUTH: Righteousness is a *heart condition*, and the goodness that comes from a changed heart. It is not something we can manufacture by trying to live up to a high moral standard (rowing). God plants His righteousness within us when we become His children, and the Spirit weaves righteousness into our heart and life as we learn to align with Him (sailing).

The "Fruit" of Legalism

- What happens when we attempt to establish righteousness by our works.
- Creates a climate of condemnation and contempt:
    - Self-Hate when you struggle.
    - Self-Righteousness when you look good.

"I found that the very commandment that was intended to bring life actually brought death" (Rom.7:10).

"The letter kills, but the Spirit gives life" (2Cor.3:6).

Legalism cannot bring life. It may help avoid certain types of behavior.

But following good rules will not change our heart. The purpose of God's standard is to show us what we <u>cannot do</u> on our own and how much we need God.

[Video: Session 5 – Part 2]

The Alternative

<u>Receive</u> what we need from God, instead of trying to <u>achieve</u> it by our effort.

This is <u>grace</u> – God doing for us and in us what we cannot do for ourselves.

Instead of trying hard to not sin, wouldn't it make more sense to engage with God in ways that allow Him to remove our propensity to sin?

Instead of trying to deny how old wounds are affecting our life, why not engage with God in ways that allow Him to heal those wounds?

Receiving is Not Passive

Grace in its most fruitful form requires our <u>consent</u> and <u>cooperation</u>, just as sailing takes effort, but very different from the effort of rowing.

"Grace is not opposed to effort for the purpose of growth ...
  It is only opposed to earning or achieving our spiritual growth" (Dallas Willard).

Grace differs from legalism in that we <u>receive</u> what we cannot do for ourselves.

But grace does not mean we are passive in how we engage with God.

One of the most misunderstood aspects of grace is the matter regarding how human beings are involved in the process.

Does it cease to be grace if there is something we must do?

Grace Makes Truth Possible

Grace is what makes it <u>safe:</u>

• To know the truth of who we are.
• To know where we are in the process.
• To be fully known.

The psalmist feels *safe to be known and loved* at the same time.

"Search me, O God" (Ps.139).

In no way does this ignore sin. The exact opposite is true. Grace makes it safe enough to be transparent before God so He can dig a lot deeper than we can with our own logic and wisdom. He can remove the *causes* of sin as well as cleanse us from it. God does this with love, just as a parent would take care of a sick or hurt child.

Grace is Relational

• Grace means we get the relationship first.

"But God, who is rich in mercy, out of the great love with which he loved us even when we were dead ... made us alive together with Christ – by grace you have been saved" (Eph.2:4-5 NRSV).

God did not say, "When you get cleaned up we can have a relationship." He said, "I want a relationship with you. And this relationship will be the context for your restoration."

• Grace means we can move toward God in our moment of need.

"God understands our weakness ... we find grace to help in time of need" (Heb.4:15).

> When we are lost or broken, we don't need to be told we are bad;
> we need to be told we are loved, we are worth fighting for, and
> that we matter to the kingdom and to others around us (this is Grace).

• Grace means the relationship depends on God's character,
   not on our performance.

Grace is the Means for Change

• Consider the following passages as they describe the work God does **in** us.

"This is the covenant I will make with the house of Israel after that time, declares the Lord. <u>I will put my laws in their minds and write them on their hearts</u>. I will be their God, and they will be my people" (Heb.8:10).

> Writing laws on our hearts and minds is an act of God, not something we try to achieve.

"For what the law could not do, weak as it was through the flesh, <u>God did</u>" (Rom.8:3).

> Living by rules did not work. So God made it possible to *receive*
> righteousness instead of earning it or achieving it.

"If by means of the Spirit you put to death the deeds of the body, you will live" (Rom.8:13).

> We tend to gloss over the phrase "by the Spirit" and think, "How do I put the flesh to death?" But it actually reads, "By means of the Spirit" the misdeeds of the body are destroyed.

• Grace is God's work in us to change our heart and transform our life.
   And that is <u>His</u> job, something only <u>He</u> can do.
   The Christian life is not a test we need to pass.
   It is a relationship with God who is at work in us!

One of the most serious misunderstandings of grace is that a grace-based message is soft on sin. But grace does not gloss over our sin – it eradicates sin!

Spiritual Growth – How?

There are two main approaches to spiritual growth:
- **Law** – attempting to achieve an ideal standard by direct effort.
- **Grace** – engaging with the Holy Spirit so God can change us.

This is the difference between rowing and sailing.

The key to spiritual growth is <u>learning how to engage with God</u> in ways that allow Him to change our heart.

Summary – What is Grace?

Every aspect of God's mission to overturn evil in us and in the world.
- **Who** He Is – God's nature is to rescue and restore that which He loves.
- **How** He Acts – God pursues us with love and compassion.
- **What** He Does – God does in us and for us what we cannot do.

Trying to do God's part in our renewal process will only lead to disappointment and failure. The Christian life is not about what we can do for God, it is about what He can do for us and in us. This is <u>grace</u> at work.

Why is Legalism so Common?

There are a lot of reasons why legalism as defined here is so common. First, it is natural for us to try hard to be good Christians because that is how we become good at almost everything else in life – by trying our best. It can take a while for us to grasp the "great reversal" in God's Kingdom, where things work differently from the way they do in the world. Discovering how God does in us what we cannot do for ourselves is one of these hard lessons, one we need to experience in order to really "get."

We can also find ourselves embroiled in legalism because we want to be all God wants us to be and want to please God with our lives. We may have very good intentions about living out the gospel and do not mean to become legalistic at all. But if we have never been shown any other way to grow and change, trying hard to follow good teaching may be the only approach we can come up with.

Sometimes though, we become legalistic because of poor theology or a poor image of God. If I feel a lot of shame about how I think God sees me, or if I feel as if I need to win God's approval or that I am measured by my performance, then I may try to force the "right" actions I think a Christian ought to have in order to feel less shame. But once I discover God is delighted to work with me no matter how messed up I am, those reasons for shame become meaningless.

Some people believe very strongly that following rules is the only way to stay "pure." After all, if we do not have standards to follow, who knows what will happen. We need to control our dark side so it does not run loose. But these fears are based on a weak understanding of how God works in our lives, which leads us to our final thought.

The biggest reason we fall back on a legalistic approach to spiritual growth, is that people have not yet discovered the <u>power of Grace</u> within the context of an interactive, authentic relationship with God. Once we know how God changes lives, then we know how to receive what we need in order to become more whole, instead of trying to crank it out on our own. We learn to live in grace!

Exercise 5B – Incorporating More Grace Into My Life

For this exercise we are going to spend some time talking to God about an area in our life where we need to experience more of God's work and less of our own direct effort.

1. Ask God if there is one area below He would like to talk to you about.
2. Spend some time reflecting and listening to what God wants to reveal to you about this matter.
3. Use the space below to write out your reflection and any thoughts revealed by God.

   • Is there an area in my life that I have been expecting to correct on my own?
   • Are there ways I have been expecting my knowledge of doctrine or my involvement in the church to make me a better Christian? How would living by grace impact any of this process?
   • Is there another person I have judged too harshly? God, how do You see this person?
   • God, is there something I have felt too ashamed of to talk to You about? What do I need to know about You that will change how I think You see me?

Session 5 Sailing Practice – Ongoing

1. Focus on the goodness of God each morning and night (Appreciating the Goodness of God).
2. Listen to the Spirit teach you about abiding in John 14-15 (Directly Interacting).

Session 5 Sailing Practice – More Grace

Choose another item from Exercise 5B and do this exercise again.
— and/or —
If something comes up during the week for which you need a change of heart, seek God and ask Him for grace – for Him to do in you what you cannot do, so you can address the situation through a changed heart and the eyes of heaven.

Remember when you ask God to do a work of Grace in you, that means you are ready to engage with Him further and to join Him in searching your heart for what you need. This is not about passively waiting for Him to "fix" you.

No matter what we have to deal with, we can always ask God what we are missing, because we are always missing something! As we see life through His eyes, our heart will change. We can then live differently from the way we did before. The key is to seek Him out and engage with Him directly about our life so He can do His work.

Additional Reading on Grace as a Means for Change

Steve McVey: *Grace Walk: What You've Always Wanted in the Christian Life* (Harvest House: Eugene, OR) 2005

Ship's Log – Session 5

I think *grace* was one of the most difficult Kingdom lessons for me to really grasp. When I read about the great heroes of Christian history, I noticed they often described in great detail how they discovered the secret of receiving life from God instead of cranking it out on their own. That all sounded great, but I was still left with the question, "How does a normal person like me find what *they* found? What does it mean to *receive* what I need for life?"

One thing I am now sure of is that we will never make sense of this by studying the idea more thoroughly. This is something we need to <u>experience</u> first-hand. Otherwise, it is too far removed from our everyday life to make any sense. It's a little like trying to comprehend a jogger's "high" when the most I have ever run is a couple of blocks before feeling totally exhausted and out of breath. Or maybe a better metaphor would be that of trying to imagine true love – joyful, reciprocating, mutual love – if all I've ever known is broken relationships and heartbreak. I might even resent the idea that such a life is possible, let alone the fact that I can never seem to find it.

It bears asking again. How do we "receive" the goodness we need in order to live more fully? How can the Christian life be more than a resolution or a commitment to try harder? I know these questions haunted me for many years, and I know some of you who are reading this now have the same kind of questions. So let me see if I can offer you some hope and at least point you in a direction that makes some sense of all this.

First, if you are among those whose hearts were lifted during the previous sessions on hearing God and having conversations with Him, you now know experientially how God can speak into your life and impact your soul by doing so. This is the very essence of how we receive life from God. When He reveals something to me I have not seen before, it gives me a comfort and peace I cannot describe, even if what He reveals to me are things about my heart I would rather not see. The truth really does set us free. And when He speaks to me about some painful memories and shows me what I need to know about them, my pain diminishes so much I can hardly believe the lightness it gives to my soul. He has such an amazing way of telling my story and clearing up the misinterpretations I have of my own life, that those difficult things let go of their grip on me and I let go of my grip on the pain. That is God doing for me what I cannot do.

For those of you who are having difficulty hearing God or feeling connected to Him, I would encourage you to continue practicing spiritual reflection and the other appreciation exercises outlined throughout this course. Spending time with God and focusing our mind on the good things He has given to us and on the ways He loves us can have a far deeper impact than one might think. If we give ourselves to these things, both body and soul, we will discover the joy of being changed in ways we would not have thought possible otherwise. This will then build a bridge to discerning the movements of the Spirit.

My deepest hope and prayer is that you will truly come to know the joy of <u>receiving</u> what we cannot do for ourselves! May God richly bless your time with Him.

David Takle
Sailor Apprentice

SESSION 6 – ENGAGING WITH GOD FOR CHANGE (PART 1)
BALANCING GOD'S PART AND OUR PART

So far we have established that spiritual growth comes from God rather than from trying hard to do the right things. We have also spent some time practicing conversational prayer as a way of engaging with God. We now turn our attention to some of the other ways we can connect with God that will foster our growth and character formation.

Historically, these ways of spending time with God have been referred to as *spiritual disciplines*. We almost hesitate to use this phrase, however, because there is so much baggage associated with the word "disciplines." People have often found spiritual practices to be difficult and dry, or even legalistic in nature, so it may sound strange to speak of them as life-giving.

There are two major reasons why we do not find these practices as helpful as we might hope. First, these practices have often been taught as if they are simply *tasks* we should do. What we hear is that there are even more things we are supposed to be doing, and it makes us tired just to think about them. Second, these exercises have often been taught and practiced in an imbalanced manner, expecting spiritual growth to happen more or less automatically as a result of doing them. When people engage in spiritual practices from this perspective, they usually experience very little, if any, change. As a result, they either dismiss spiritual practices as less than helpful, or else think there is something wrong with themselves for not getting much out of the process.

Our goal in this session is to explain the true nature of spiritual practices and what makes the difference between going through the motions of a dead practice and having a life-giving experience with God. How we understand and engage in spiritual practices makes a tremendous difference in the kind of fruit they bear in our lives. And please note we are not talking about approaching these practices with a "better attitude," but using them with a fundamentally different focus and purpose.

We will also introduce a model which divides spiritual practices into two groups: those which focus on appreciating God's goodness and presence, and those in which we interact directly with God. Conversational prayer is a primary example of direct interaction, whereas practices of appreciation offer a number of ways of engaging with God that are not centered around hearing God (although we may still ask Him for insight and comfort). We hope the value of this model will become more clear as we proceed.

As we learn how to use these practices in a balanced manner to connect more deeply with God, we will experience both short term and long term benefits. In the short term, *appreciation* practices increase our awareness of God's presence with us, build our trust in His goodness toward us, and strengthen our relational bond with Him. *Directly interacting* with God usually provides more insight into the spiritual realities of our life, and allows God to speak into places in our life that need change. In the long term, we train our heart to expect God's real presence in our life and to turn to Him often, in good times and bad. Above all, we learn how to walk with Him and live in Him.

[Video: Session 6 – Part 1]

Engaging With God is Primary

Our primary means for spiritual growth is always ***connecting with God***
    not "obedience" or any other "spiritual" activity.

Connecting with God is the basis for what God wants to do

• To renew our heart.
    – Engaging with God is life-changing in itself.
    – What our heart truly needs we can only receive from Him.
• To grow a multi-generational people of God (Eph.2:19-22).
    – With spiritual elders, parents, brothers, sisters, children all working together, some upstream from us and some downstream.

You may have been taught the main avenues of spiritual growth are:
    obedience, accountability, getting into ministry, Bible study.

But growth is primarily based on the quality of our relationship with God and our relationships with other members of the Body of Christ.

Balancing God's Part and Our Part

Question: "Why do you suppose we have trouble seeing a direct link between fasting and spiritual health?"

• Spiritual practices DO NOT change us!
    They only make a space for engaging with God.[4]
    This is one of the most important things to know about spiritual practices.
• Misunderstanding and misusing spiritual practices, expecting them to change us simply because we do them is the main reason why people give up on them.
• Misusing spiritual practices will cause them to become dry and lifeless.
• Remember grace (what God does in us) is not opposed to effort, but it is opposed to earning or achieving.
    – Spiritual practices do require effort, usually involving our entire body.
    – Engaging with God requires some effort on our part.
    – But that effort *does not* change our heart.
        It is simply the effort we employ to make a space for engaging with God.
    – We are changed by engaging with Him.

If we read our Bible month after month expecting our effort to change us, we can get discouraged because the act of reading is not sufficient to change us very much. But if reading the Bible is used as a springboard for time with God, the whole process is radically changed into a relational experience in which we can become active participants with Him in His work in our life.

---

4 Dallas Willard: *The Spirit of the Disciplines*

God's Part – as Our Mentor and Only Source of Life

- To <u>be with</u> us – conscious awareness of His presence gives us life.
- Reveal Himself to us – His love, His presence, His intentions for us.
- Reveal our heart – good things of God, as well as things that need changing.
- Speak truth – God's perspective on our life will set us free.
- Heal and renew – what God can do as we learn to participate.

Jesus did <u>not</u> finish training His disciples in 3 years. He gave us the Holy Spirit to pick up where He left off. The Holy Spirit loves to mentor!

Our Part – as an Apprentice (Student) of Jesus

- Deliberately engage – persistently give Him our time and focused attention.
- Remain teachable – we are students of a life we know very little about.
     Kingdom life is not at all intuitive. We need continuous help.
- Listen, observe, ask questions – we are actively engaged, not passive.
- Receive – life comes from God, not from our activity.

Learning <u>how to receive</u> from God is one of our greatest challenges!

Remember, God loves to give good gifts to His children (Isa.55).

[Video: Session 6 – Part 2]

Making Space to Engage With God

	With Myself (solitude)	**With Others** (community)
Appreciating	Private Worship Spiritual Reflection Abstaining / Extending	Appreciation Stories Service to Others Recovery Support
Interacting	Listening to the Word Dialogue Repentance	Encouragement Healing Prayer Forgiveness

We can use a variety of spiritual practices to set aside time and make a space where we can focus our attention on God and participate in His work to fill our heart with His love and truth, to disarm our fears and mistaken ideas about life, and to heal the broken places in our heart.

We will look at a few spiritual practices in this session and the next two:
- Why they are helpful.
- How they can be life-giving.
- Why they often turn into things that weigh us down.
- The difference between life-giving practices and draining disciplines.

Spending Time With God

We have two main ways of engaging with God:

- <u>Interacting</u> directly
  - Conversations with God that allow Him to minister directly to us through speaking, showing, revealing.
  - We can receive new perspectives and healing during our interaction.
- <u>Appreciating</u> God's goodness and presence
  - Accept by faith that He is with us no matter what, and allow ourselves to feel gratitude for His presence and for what He has done in us.
  - Our trust will grow, and we will internalize His presence over time.

Appreciation Moment

Any practice that seeks to reflect on God, His presence, and/or His goodness.

These are ways we can engage with God apart from conversational prayer.

Many of these practices can be viewed as <u>spiritual exercises</u> for the soul.

Our intention is to identify and practice ways that:

- Strengthen our bond with Him.
- Lead to greater comfort and security in Him.
- Create greater appreciation for Him.
- Build bridges to interacting directly with Him.

"Think on these things" (Phil.4:8).   "Always giving thanks" (Eph.5:20).

We tend to underestimate the value of appreciation in building relationship.

Variety is also very helpful here – using these practices to build joy with God, and not merely going through the motions of a spiritual exercise.

There are two main approaches to practicing appreciation:

- <u>Appreciation in Joy:</u> when we can readily feel or experience His goodness.
- <u>Appreciation in Distress:</u> when something stands between us and joy.

Practicing <u>Appreciation in Joy</u> for God's Presence and Goodness

1. Turn the eyes of your heart toward God.
2. Bring to mind something of value for which you are grateful.
3. Spend time with Him
   - in a place of appreciation for God's gift to you.
   - resting in His presence and His goodness.

This has been one of our on-going Sailing Practices since Session 2.

Examples of some ways to "Practice appreciating the presence of God":

- Go for a walk and allow the beauty of creation to impact you.
- Write out a psalm of praise.
- Remember an experience for which you are grateful.
- Put on a favorite CD and sing from your heart to God.
- Simply notice by faith that He is with you.

Exercise 6A – Practicing Appreciation in Joy

"Be filled with the Spirit, speaking to one another in psalms and hymns and spiritual songs, singing and making melody with your heart to the Lord; always giving thanks for all things in the name of our Lord Jesus Christ" (Eph.5:18-20, NASB).

This will be a fairly short exercise of quieting and focusing. Our goal here is to become more aware of God's presence with us and to appreciate His goodness toward us. As we begin to feel gratitude and joy, we want to simply enjoy our closeness with God.

- Accept in faith that God's presence is completely enveloping you at this moment, permeating every cell of your body.
- Turn your heart toward Him as you quiet your mind.
- Envision God enjoying this moment with you.
- Allow yourself to rejoice in His presence and goodness.

Enjoy the moment!

(If several minutes pass without any sense of appreciation, reflect back on a prior time when you aware of the presence of God, and allow yourself to feel appreciation for that experience).

Notes   **[Video: Session 6 – Part 3]**

Seeking <u>Appreciation from a Place of Distress</u>

We can learn to seek appreciation even in times of distress.

This is probably the most common form of the Psalms (called psalms of lament).

- Declaring to God as honestly as I can …
    What I think I know, what I do not know, and what feels true.
    Honestly – not attempting to sanitize my discussion with God.
- Some particular area of my life …
    Sharing with God my "red dot."[5] ("You are here.")
    What is on my heart, my thoughts and feelings.
    Example: Psalm 13.
- Allowing Him to minister to me …
    Knowing He is good, He is present with me, and He is always ready to listen.
    Knowing He is abundantly able to restore me.
    Psalms of Lament often express this kind of expectation.
- Bringing me comfort …
    Because He is with me.
    Because He listens to my story.
    Because He knows how to comfort me.
    Because He can show me how He sees my situation.
- Leading me into appreciation.
    A natural result of taking my burdens to God.

Examples of Appreciation in "Psalms of Lament (Distress)"
    (Ps. 3, 13, 22, 56, 57, 61, 77, 86, 142)

<u>Great examples of bringing our laments to God, without losing hope:</u>

"To the Lord I cry aloud, and he answers me from his holy hill" (Ps.3:4).

"When I am afraid, I will trust in you" (Ps.56:3).

"I will take refuge in the shadow of your wings until the disaster has passed" (Ps.57:1).

"From the ends of the earth I call to you, I call as my heart grows faint; lead me to the rock that is higher than I" (Ps.61:2).

"When my spirit grows faint within me, it is you who knows my way" (Ps.142:3).

---

5 The "Red Dot" image comes from Larry Crabb in *The Papa Prayer*

Exercise 6B – Writing a Psalm of Appreciation in Distress

While there are times when we feel appreciation quite naturally, we also have times and areas of life where we do not feel at all appreciative. We find this to be true in the Psalms, as well. This exercise will begin with an area in which we feel burdened, and move toward a place of trust and comfort for which we can feel appreciation. We are not asking God to resolve any issues at this time, but to help us arrive at a place where we can appreciate His presence and goodness in the midst of our difficulty. In the process, we will write out a short Psalm that has elements of both our distress and appreciation.

1. Spend 2 minutes quieting and focusing on the presence of God.
   • If possible, find some place of appreciation (unrelated to your area of distress) that you can acknowledge and feel.

2. Spend 5 minutes writing to God about an area of distress in your life.
   • Consider asking God what area to address.
   • Work / Home / Relative / Friend / Health / Finances.
   • Include the situation, emotions, affected relationships, and whatever seems to be at stake.

3. Spend 4 minutes allowing God to restore comfort to you in whatever way He desires.
   • Actively seek His presence with you and His love for you.
   • Welcome any new perspectives He might want to show you.
   • Continue to record what comes to mind during this time.

4. Spend 2 minutes writing out your appreciation for God's response to you and His comfort.

[Video: Session 6 – Part 4]

Appreciation Stories

Sharing our stories about God's work in us in regard to:
- Comfort we have received.
- Insights we have received.
- How God is changing and healing us.
- How we have discerned His leading.

Stories communicate meaning in ways that reach the heart of both the speaker and listener. We learn from each other and are motivated to move toward God when we hear the experiences of others who have received good things from God.

Some examples:
- This is how God comforted me in my loss.
- This is what wrestling with God can look like.
- This is how God rescued me and healed me.
- This is what I discovered that I had not known before, by waiting on God.

We need to hear how God is active in the lives of others: It is encouraging; It builds our trust and confidence in God; It tells us that God is active in others around us.

Appreciation Stories

How we tell the story is important.
- When telling a story of seeking appreciation from a place of distress, we need to <u>focus on God's response to us</u>, instead of focusing on the pain.
- Goal is to help our listeners share our experience of God.
  - Emotions and how they changed when God responded.
  - Physical sensations we experienced.
  - Peace and comfort that came with God's response.
  - What it was like to sense His presence with us.
  - Insights we received.

We are not simply relating the details of our experience. Our intention here is to genuinely share with others some of what God has given to us. So when we tell the story, we want to engage our listeners as much as possible, and help them join us in our experience so they can get a real sense of what God is doing in us.

There is also a place for telling the pain side of our story, but usually with close friends or counselors. In most group settings, it is generally better to focus on the appreciation elements of our story.

Exercise 6C – Telling Our Appreciation Stories

In this exercise you will share your experience in regard to Seeking Appreciation in Distress in Exercise 6B. If you did not reach a place of appreciation during this exercise, feel free to share another experience you have had in which you were able to be comforted by God.

1. Gather in groups of 3 (or in pairs).
2. Everyone <u>tells an appreciation story</u> about how God met them in Exercise 6B.
   - About 3 minutes per person.
   - Focus on the joy part of the story. Include only a very brief reference to the type of distress.
   - Help your listeners know what it was like to experience God's comfort.
   - Include how your thoughts, emotions, and body changed as God met you.

[Video: Session 6 – Part 5]

Other Ways to Practice Appreciating God's Presence With Us

	With Myself (solitude)	**With Others** (community)
Appreciating	Private Worship Spiritual Reflection Abstaining / Extending	Appreciation Stories Service to Others Recovery Support
Interacting	Listening to the Word Dialogue Repentance	Encouragement Healing Prayer Forgiveness

Practices of Abstaining and Extending
   In addition to seeking appreciation in whatever life brings you,
   we can practice appreciation intentionally as a spiritual exercise.
   - Deliberately do something different to change your normal patterns.
   - If possible, enjoy the presence of God with you in that experience.
   - Seek appreciation in your experience (from either a place of joy or distress).

   Abstaining (removing something familiar) or **Extending** (trying something new) can create a context for stirring up deeply embedded concerns, attitudes and values, both positive and negative. By seeking appreciation intentionally in this manner, <u>we train our soul to look for God in all things</u>.

- Examples of abstaining:
  - Stop watching TV for two weeks.
  - Try saying "No" to a food craving for a few weeks (chocolate, soda, sugar).
  - Do not play video games or watch sports or whatever your favorite distraction might be.
  - Cut back on overtime or long hours at work (if applicable).
- Examples of extending:
  - Volunteer some time at a food pantry.
  - Reflect on a verse you find challenging or confronting.
  - Do something for someone else anonymously.

After (or during) any one of these changes, take the time to reflect on your internal reactions to your experience, and then walk through to a place of appreciation as we did earlier.

Remember these actions will not make you more "spiritual" by doing them, but they can open a space for engaging with God, engaging with Him for His presence and comfort in all things, by seeking a place of appreciation.

Most of all, these intentional exercises will train our heart and mind to be thankful in all things.

These practices can expose areas in our life where we need healing. We will discuss the process of inner healing in more detail in Sessions 9-10-11.

Private Worship

Singing to God with all my heart and soul.

- Engages more of the mind and heart.
- Helps us focus.

Elisha used music to help calm and focus.

"(Elisha) 'But now bring me a minstrel.' And it came about, when the minstrel played, that the hand of the LORD came upon him" (2Kings.3:15).

Idea: Create CD's or play lists by theme.

- Songs of joy.
- Songs that speak to my identity as a child of God.
- Songs that focus on the goodness of God and His activity in my life.
- Songs to aid me in times of distress, or where I need repentance.

See "Sailing Practice" at the end of this session for a description of one way to do this practice.

Balancing God's Part and Our Part

Spiritual practices *do not* change us, they only *make a space* for encountering God, and bring focus to our desire to be with Him.

Engaging with God is what changes us.

Session 6 Sailing Practice – Ongoing

1. Focus on the goodness of God each morning and night (Appreciating the Goodness of God).
2. Listen to the Spirit teach you about abiding in John 14-15 (Directly Interacting).

Session 6 Sailing Practice 1 – Making an Appreciation List

The hardest time to recall a place of appreciation is when you are already in distress. To help you get to appreciation more easily, it is helpful to internalize a short "Appreciation List" so you do not have to try to think of something in those moments when it is difficult to do so.

- Create a list of 3 to 5 things for which you feel a great deal of appreciation.
  – identify people, experiences, healings, etc. (no material items except for restored necessities).
- Give each item on the list a short name (e.g. "Wedding Day" or "2001 Road Trip").
- Memorize the List.
- Bring the list to mind each morning as you wake up and turn your mind toward the goodness of God. Recall the name of each appreciation moment and give yourself a minute to reflect on what that name means to you.

Session 6 Sailing Practice 2 – Private Worship

Choose a time when you are home alone. Put a favorite CD on and allow yourself to be moved by the music. Sing, dance, and enjoy the presence of God. Play the really good songs more than once. Embrace any feelings of joy, gratitude, warmth, etc. If you are moved by grief or another difficult emotion, talk to God about it and perhaps write out what is going on inside you and ask God to reveal what you need from Him. Then re-engage with songs of joy and appreciation. When you are done, spend a few minutes in total silence, being quiet with God and appreciating your time together.

Additional Reading on Spiritual Practices

Dallas Willard: *The Spirit of the Disciplines: Understanding How God Changes Lives* (HarperOne: New York) 1990

Jan Johnson: *When the Soul Listens* (NavPress: Colorado Springs) 1999

Ship's Log – Session 6

I want to go on record here with two of the most important appreciation stories of my life. While there are many stories I could tell about how God has healed my heart, these represent some of the more dramatic moments of my life.

When I was about 31 years old, a number of areas in my life that I had been trying to cope with for a long time began to unravel. By the time I was 34, I was deeply depressed, feeling very hopeless and abandoned by God and everyone else. I remember one day finally crying out to God in my distress and confessing to Him from my heart, "God, whatever it is that I am doing ... it's not working."

What happened next is a little difficult to describe. There was no fanfare, no angel or voice from heaven. I simply saw in my mind's eye an image of a tiny light, shining at the far end of a very long tunnel. It was the ray of hope I was looking for – a metaphor so real that it got all the way into my heart. "It's going to be all right," was the only thought in my mind, and a peace came over me that I can only attribute to God. I can only describe it as the kind of calm you might feel after a great storm has passed, and you realize it's finally over. You can begin again. There is sunlight shining through the clouds here and there, and you are going to be all right.

In many ways, nothing had changed. All the things in my life that were messed up were still there, with all the problems they presented. But somehow I knew deep in my soul these were all bits and pieces that would someday be resolved. The important thing was that I was alive and I had hope. Within a few short weeks I was heavily involved in a support group that became an important part of my healing.

I love that story, because it was there that I experienced one of the most dramatic transforming moments of my life. I am totally grateful and amazed at what God can do to reveal life and hope in such dark places. I know what it is like to carry my lament to God and find almost no resolution at all at the time, other than His companionship and comfort.

My wedding day comes to mind as a second example. In the Spring of 1991, when Jan and I were finding so much joy and healing as we planned our wedding, I was deeply hurt by the response of my mother and some of my siblings to our engagement. As the wedding approached, I needed to find a way to deal with my grief so that I could fully celebrate and enjoy our wedding day. When Jan and I turned to our counselor for help, he carefully showed us how we could hold joy and grief together at the same time without ruining our joy or denying our grief. That was the revelation we needed. As we then leaned on God for His support and love, we found that we could indeed cry out to Him in our distress and at the same time rejoice in His presence with us and the comfort He offered us. By fully *embracing* our distress and bringing it to God so we could receive His care, we experienced far more joy on that day than if we had tried to *deny* our sadness.

I think that was the secret the psalmists knew, and why they could sing for joy in the midst of their laments. Seeking God, we can experience His love and comfort even when life is difficult. For that I am truly grateful.

David Takle
Sailor Apprentice

SESSION 7 – ENGAGING WITH GOD FOR CHANGE (PART 2)
WHAT TO EXPECT WHEN ENGAGING WITH GOD

We have been talking a lot about engaging with God for change. But what kinds of things can we expect to happen during the process? Are there some common elements that most Christians experience when engaging with God? What can we expect from Him? What might happen inside us? These are some of the questions we will try to address in this session.

Many Christians today have fairly low expectations of their "Quiet Time" and may have given up on it because the effort has seemed to be disproportionately high in comparison to the fruit. We have already talked about the main reasons for this:
1. An imbalance between our part and God's part, leading to disillusionment.
2. An expectation that "doing" a spiritual practice should make a difference simply because we did it.

Whenever we have faulty expectations of how God will work in our life, we are set up for disappointment that may hurt us deeply and have very serious consequences for our spiritual journey. For example, if we are sitting quietly and waiting passively for God to interrupt the silence with His voice, there is a good chance that we will be left empty handed because that is not how God usually speaks to us. We could easily misinterpret that experience and say we are unable to hear from God, when the real problem is that we need to adjust some of our expectations about how God speaks.

On the other hand, accurate expectations will prepare us to notice what God is doing. If we know God likes to reveal new perspectives about our lives, it encourages us to be more persistent in searching for the gems we need from Him. If we are anticipating an encounter with God Himself, our heart will be far more receptive and ready to notice God's presence with us, and we will look for the Author of those words on the page.

In addition to cultivating good expectations of our times with God, we need to maintain a proper balance between God's part and our part in the process. This goes back to our discussion of grace as well. If I take on too much of the work of spiritual growth, I end up with either an overdose of self-righteousness or a lot of shame about not being able to pull it off. On the other hand, if I am too passive in the process, expecting God to transform me without any effort on my part, I will probably end up disillusioned with either God or myself or both.

Knowing what we can expect from our time with God allows us to anticipate God's goodness. As we engage with Him, we begin to look for those things that we know characterize the way He interacts with us. That expectation is itself a form of faith in Him that gives us the desire to invest our whole self in the process. We listen better, pay attention more closely, and focus our participation in the right directions.

Knowing what to look for also improves our discernment. Rabbit trails start to look more like the distractions they really are, and true, live-giving, tailor-made revelations of life become more visible even in the early stages of our awareness of them. Our hope is that this session will be an encouragement, by casting a vision of what to expect and increasing our expectations of those gifts.

Discussion – What has been your experience so far?

From our exercises so far, what can you say about what we can expect when we engage with God? What have you experienced during these exercises?
- Spiritual reflection (single word, phrase, image).
- Conversational prayer (asking questions, discussing life issues with God).
- Listening to the Word (allowing God to teach us the Word).
- Practicing appreciation (both direct appreciation and seeking it from distress).
- Private worship.

Have you sensed God's presence or love? Have you received any new insights? Have you experienced any shifts in your thoughts or attitudes?

[Video: Session 7 – Part 1]

Expect Surprises

Given that we are in relationship with an infinite God, we can expect to be surprised by what we see or hear, as well as by our process as we engage with Him.

- Being led in unexpected directions.
  - Approaching God about one thing and end up talking about another.
  - Listening to God in the Word can lead to surprising places.
- A variety of communication styles.
  - Receiving words / pictures / experiences / metaphors.
  - Dialoguing (asking questions, etc).
  - Receiving first-person impressions from God.
  - Being quiet together.
- Seeing new significance in familiar ideas.
  - For example, how much He loves me, or my need to trust Him.
- Receiving fresh insights about God, self, and life.
  - God-sight: seeing life through the eyes of heaven.
  - God's ways are higher than our ways, so there is always more.

Over time we can learn the difference between a leading and a distraction.

Expect Internal Ambivalence or Resistance

Given our unfinished spiritual condition, we often withdraw from what God wants to show us. This includes **resistance to:**
- Spending the time that it takes to be with God.
- Actually engaging with God (for various reasons).
- Specific phrases of Scripture we have trouble believing or accepting.
- What God wants to do in us.

Resistance often takes the form of a sense of disbelief or discouragement.
Resistance is a God-sized problem – Take everything back to Him.

We do not need to be alarmed by our resistance to God. We really should expect to encounter it, since we all have areas of our life that have not yet come into alignment with what God is doing in us. Our job is to notice those places where we are ambivalent and take them God for His help.

Notes

Expect Confrontation

- God wants to renew our mind, and to do that He may need to challenge us.
- Generally, God's confrontations will be non-condemning, but revealing:
  - What is in our heart that we may not even know about.
  - Ways we injure ourself and others.
  - Good things we are missing.

We need to bring these areas back to God for His help in changing our heart.

Expect a Deeper Relationship With God

Relationship is dynamic, not static like an agreed-upon contract.

- Getting to <u>know</u> God experientially.
  - Beyond knowing *about* God.
  - Discovering His heart for us (experiencing His goodness).
  - *How* He reveals, confronts and corrects.
- Building stronger awareness of His presence.
  - Learning to abide in Christ.
- Building deeper trust.
  - Our trust is probably weaker than we think.
  - Many of our problems come down to an issue of trust.
- Discovering more joy. God is glad to be with me all the time.
  - Even when I'm hard to be around.
  - Even when I don't like myself.
  - Even when I'm wrong.

The more we experience God and go deeper in our relationship with Him, the more we find our hearts changing – wanting to be more like Him, wanting to be with Him, and so on. And since God is infinite, our relationship with Him can continue to grow for the rest of our life.

What to Expect

- Engaging with God is a very dynamic, experiential learning process requiring persistence, discernment, and submission.
- This is a mentoring relationship with God.
- Process everything with God, rather than trying to figure it out it on your own.

Exercise 7 – Reading With Expectation

Enjoy a few minutes <u>Listening to the Word</u>, while fully appreciating His presence with you and anticipating His interaction with you.

- Find a place of appreciation and hold that for a full minute.
- Prayerfully anticipate that God intends for this passage to be food for your soul.
- Read through the passage below slowly (at least twice) with the expectation that you will experience:
  - Paul's hope for you as a Christian.
  - Fresh insights about God, life, or yourself.
  - Internal resistance or confrontation.
  - Deeper yearning for a stronger relationship.
- Some things you might pay attention to and discuss with God:
  - Any word or phrase that catches your attention.
  - Reactions in your body (emotional, physical).
  - Any longings that are stirred up in you.
  - Any leading or change of direction you feel drawn to.

Begin writing as you reflect and listen.

"That He would grant you, according to the riches of his glory, to be strengthened with might through his Spirit in the inner man, that Christ may dwell in your hearts through faith; that you, being rooted and grounded in love, may be able to comprehend with all the saints what is the width and length and depth and height – to know the love of Christ which passes knowledge; that you may be filled with all the fullness of God. Now to Him who is able to do exceedingly abundantly above all that we ask or think, according to the power that works in us" (Eph.3:16-20, NKJV).

[Video: Session 7 – Part 2]

Spending Time With God

Two main ways of making space to engage with God.
- Appreciating God's goodness and presence.
- Interacting directly with Him.

Making Space to Engage With God – Directly Interacting

	With Myself (solitude)	**With Others** (community)
Appreciating	Private Worship Spiritual Reflection Abstaining / Extending	Appreciation Stories Service to Others Recovery Support
Interacting	Listening to the Word Dialogue Repentance	Healing Prayer Encouragement Forgiveness

Encouragement[6]

Pointing one another back to God.
- Reminders of the unseen reality all around us.
- Reminders of our true heart.
- Calling attention to God at work in us and how He sees us.
- Need to both receive and give encouragement.

When we see God at work in another person, it is good to call attention to that and acknowledge its value. When others affirm us in this way, we get an outside confirmation that God is at work in us and giving life to others through us.

Example: "When you [something] I felt ministered to by God."

Example: "Your story of God's action in your life really ministered to my heart."

Example: "I was encouraged by your words today. I'm sure you were led by God."

Why did we list <u>encouragement</u> as a way of interacting directly with God?

Because even though we are capable of offering encouragement to one another in our own wisdom, learning how to pay attention to the Spirit of God and see what He sees in those around us allows us to express God's heart for one another.

---

6   This approach to encouragement was inspired by Larry Crabb in *Connecting*

Forgiveness

Engaging with God to restore our heart to a place of love and forgiveness
that we can extend to another person.

Instead of saying the words "I forgive you," what if we engage with God so that He can change our heart so we actually forgive the person?

- Forgiveness can be a process, rather than one of these extremes:
  – Forgiving too easily (dismissive, ignoring our true feelings).
  – Refusing to forgive (resistant, getting stuck in our feelings).
- Ways in which forgiveness can be a process:
  – It requires a change of heart that comes from engaging with God.
  – We may need to address a problem more than once, due to multiple injuries.
- Elements of forgiveness:
  – Seeing other people through the eyes of heaven.
  – Receiving our own change of heart about them.
  – Releasing the debt they "owe" us.

These are all steps that we need God's help with.

Also, forgiveness does not depend on other people changing or making restitution. It is letting go of any conviction that they "owe me" something, whether or not they offer restitution.

Important: If we expect others to *earn* forgiveness from us, we will have a hard time receiving forgiveness from God when we need it. We will either feel that we have to earn it (perhaps by feeling sorry enough), or else we will be guilty of a double standard whereby we want forgiveness but do not offer it to others.

Repentance

Engaging with God for a change of heart
that is deeper than we are capable of on our own.

Many people think repentance is *a change of heart that we make* and then express to God. What if we *engaged with God for a change of heart* that is deeper than we are capable of on our own?

There is much within us that we cannot change by willpower.

Consider Psalm 51, "Create in me a clean heart, renew a right spirit within me." David did not simply make a resolution to be good or to try harder, he asked God to do a work in him so he could become the person he wanted to be.

"God, I do not want to be like this. Begin Your work in me and show me how to participate with You in order to be changed."

- Not a resolution that we try to make.
- Agreeing with God that we need a change of heart.
- A change of heart that comes from God, not achieved by our own effort.
- Non-condemning (even if it is hard for us to face).
- Repentance can be the start of a process of change.

Session 7 Sailing Practice – Ongoing

1. Focus on the goodness of God each morning and night (Appreciating the Goodness of God).
2. Listen to the Spirit teach you about abiding in John 14-15 (Directly Interacting).

Session 7 Sailing Practice 1 – Encouragement

1. Ask God to bring to mind someone you appreciate for the good you have received from that person.
2. Ask God to help you put into words what you appreciate about that person.
3. Make a point to tell the person what you see in them. This can be done in person, by sending a card, by making a phone call, or whatever.

Session 7 Sailing Practice 2 – Forgiveness

1. Ask God to bring to mind someone you have not forgiven for something.
2. Write out your resentments, your feelings, your anger.
3. Ask God to help you go beyond what you have written and show you how He sees the other person and the hurt you have experienced. Write out whatever He reveals to you.
4. Ask God to move your heart toward forgiveness.
5. Record any changes you experience during this conversation.

Session 7 Sailing Practice 3 – Repentance

1. Ask God to bring to mind an area in which you need to change your attitude or behavior.
2. Ask Him to show you more of your heart and any reasons why you might have remained stuck or unwilling to change so far.
3. Confess your desire for change.
4. Ask Him to reveal what you need from Him in order to become more of the person you want to be.
5. Write out your thoughts as you listen to Him.

Additional Reading on Spiritual Practices

Dallas Willard: *The Spirit of the Disciplines: Understanding How God Changes Lives* (HarperOne: New York) 1990

Jan Johnson: *When the Soul Listens* (NavPress: Colorado Springs) 1999

Ship's Log – Session 7

Much of my life I lived in Minnesota, where we experienced four very distinct seasons each year. As a child, I often thought that when the snow melted away it meant spring had arrived, only to be disappointed when we had yet another snowfall. Eventually, I learned that the presence or absence of snow was not a very good measure of the change of seasons. A far better indicator was when the robins began to come back from their southern home. Sometime around March each year, we would begin to pay attention to the birds we saw, expecting to see a robin. Sooner or later we would spot one, and then we would know Spring had finally arrived – even if there was a late snow.

On another note, for many years I longed to experience God's presence, but I was repeatedly let down because He never seemed to show up. There were no bright lights or majestic visions, and no booming voice in my head. I kept looking for something really spectacular along the lines of the most dramatic stories I could find in the Bible about God showing up and overwhelming people. But none of those things happened. It was like wanting all the snow to melt, when I should have been looking for robins.

Once I was shown more about what to expect, I knew better what to look for and could begin to anticipate God's presence and listen for His voice with far more confidence and expectation than I had before. And as my relationship with God has grown, He has continued to shape my expectations in order to broaden my experience of Him and the ways in which He can be with me.

For example, most of my encounters with God in early 2000 had to do with healing my identity and some of the emotional scars I had been carrying around all my life. I was amazed at how much God wanted to restore me and how wonderfully good He was at the whole process of restoring my heart. At one point, I started expecting every worthwhile encounter with God to include some level of healing. If that did not happen, I was often disappointed and felt like something was wrong. Gently, God began to show me that in addition to restoring the bad things in my life, He also wanted to bring forward movement to my life in very positive ways. He wanted to Mentor me about daily life in His Kingdom. So then my expectations shifted toward being taught by Him every time we engaged in conversation, resorting to healing only when it seemed appropriate in the context of what He was showing me. Over time, I began to assume that any good conversation had to include some high-quality mentoring. If that did not happen, I would once again be disappointed with my quiet time. When I finally asked Him why some of these conversations seemed so "flat," He revealed that He often wants me to spend time with Him for the sake of appreciating His presence and receiving His love and comfort, and nothing more.

I think I am finally getting the picture, that God has many ways to be with us and many ways to feed our soul. He may teach us about life, He may speak into a wounded place, He may want us to experience more of His love, or He might simply want to be with us in ways we are more conscious of at the moment. So my expectations keep growing, along with my experience of how He might want to reveal Himself to me. The more I learn about what to look for, the more I see Him and experience His presence in my life. Perhaps the greatest lesson of all has been that He is closer to me than my own breath. And that is why, more and more, I expect to encounter Him in the very moment I turn my eyes toward Him.

David Takle
Sailor Apprentice

SESSION 8 – ENGAGING WITH GOD FOR CHANGE (PART 3)
BARRIERS TO ENGAGING WITH GOD

Connecting with God is not always easy. Sometimes He feels a million miles away. Other times it seems like we are hemmed in by a brick wall and nothing gets past it, either way. How can we learn to identify these barriers better, and what can we do about them?

Barriers can be very painful for two reasons. First, if we cannot connect well with God, we are left to our own resources to deal with life. And all through this course we have emphasized the fact that our own resources will never restore our soul or grow us up into the people God created us to be. The second reason barriers can be painful is that the loss of relationship with God is distressing in and of itself. We are designed to live in relationship to God just as much as we are designed to drink water and breathe air.

This is why it is important to know when we are bumping up against a barrier and why we need to know some ways to address them fairly directly. Many times we think our only recourse is to hang on and hope the barrier goes away. But because God is so relational, we have possibilities available to us that would not otherwise be the case.

Barriers to God come in many forms. **Cognitive** barriers have to do with poor theology and mistaken ideas about who God is. For example, if we believe that God should protect us from anything painful in this world, sooner or later we will feel betrayed by Him. Our poor theology becomes a barrier. Throughout this course we have made a point of identifying popular misconceptions about the Christian life, because changes in how we see the Kingdom can make the difference between being stuck and moving on.

We also encounter **spiritual** barriers from time to time. These have to do with demonic forces that seek to interrupt our relationship with God. Our enemy has a vested interest in keeping us from finding the life we see in the New Testament. As with other areas of Christian living, there is a lot of confusion and poor theology regarding how we should deal with this area. Our best recourse is to build a robust relationship with God and learn to rely on Him for discernment and answers to spiritual barriers.

Developmental barriers can also inhibit our spiritual growth. These barriers come from not having a strong community around us to help us mature as human beings. We will address this problem more in Session 12. For now, let us say that reaching the age of adulthood does not mean that we are functioning at an adult level, emotionally or relationally. And if we are stuck developmentally, there will probably be some limitations on our spiritual growth as well.

In this session we will focus on the most common **emotional** barriers that we face, and offer some perspectives on what lies beneath them and how to address them. Specifically, we will look at anger, fear, shame, and hopelessness, to see how they can interfere with our relationship to God and with our spiritual development. Knowing what to look for and what to do with these barriers is important, because everyone deals with one or more of these at some point along the way.

[Video: Session 8 – Part 1]

Balancing God's Part and Our Part (Session 6)

Spiritual practices do <u>not</u> change us. They make a space for encountering God.

What to Expect When Engaging With God (Session 7)

Experiential learning is a very dynamic process, requiring
    discernment, submission, and persistence.
Process everything with God.

Barriers Are Common (Session 8)

- We all have things that get in the way of connecting with God – sensing, seeing, hearing, and relating to God.

  "Now <u>we see things imperfectly as in a cloudy mirror</u>, but then we will see everything with perfect clarity. All that I know now is partial and incomplete" (1Cor.13:12, NLT).

- We should not be too surprised or feel uniquely defective when we discover barriers in the way. We should actually expect to find them.
- We are unfinished works of grace in a broken world. It would be very surprising if we did <u>not</u> have barriers between us and God.

Emotional Barriers

Anger / Fear / Shame / Hopelessness.
We need to be able to identify these barriers, so that we can be more purposeful in our conversations with God about the things that hinder our relationship with Him.

Anger Toward God

- Resentments that we hold in our heart in regard to:
  - Good things we think God should have done.
  - Bad things we think God should have prevented.
- Motivates us to **harden** our heart or **run** from God.
- Places us in an adversarial relationship with Him.
- Usually rooted in our expectations of how we think God should act.

Fear of God

- Common forms of anxiety we have in regard to:
  - What God might say or do to me.
  - What God might want from me or might take away from me.
  - What God might think of me.
- Fear motivates us to **protect** our heart or **avoid** God.
- Often comes from bad theology and/or distorted images of God.

Shame

- Not wanting God to see our "stuff."
  - We think He is as disappointed in us as we are.
- Difficulty dealing with shame in general.
  - Fear of making mistakes.
  - Believing that our flaws make us unacceptable. ("I need to be right.")
  - Defensive posture, self-protection.
- Motivates us to **hide** from God.
- If we are unable to deal with shame, we may be unable to engage in honest self-examination or tolerate God's light in the places He wants to restore.

Hopelessness

Disbelief due to:

- Prior experience.
  - When difficulty immediately follows victory.
  - Encountering same issue over and over without resolving very much.
- Difficulty hearing God.
  - "Fruitless" times of engaging.

Destroys our motivation and causes us to dismiss God as irrelevant. Hopelessness is a form of disbelief that becomes its own problem.

The Problem of Trust

Emotional barriers are primarily a lack of trust.

Anger: I distrust God's actions in my life.

Fear: I distrust God's intentions toward me.

Shame: I distrust God's perceptions of me.

Hopelessness: I have given up on God either restoring me or being with me.

Relationships require trust. So these issues interfere with our relationships.

Where's the problem? Either:

- God is not trustworthy.

      – or –

- My "truster" is broken.

When we get stuck in these emotions with regard to other people (rather than God), our emotional state will often interfere with <u>all</u> of our relationships, including our relationship with God. Witness the way in which a bad day can cause us to snap at people we really care about. That happens because these emotions spill over into other areas of our life. So it is very important for us to resolve these issues by taking them to God.

Given the world we live in, we would expect our "trusters" to get broken. That is one reason why God's love and goodness are so important to us. Getting to know God's character by our own direct experience of Him will build our trust.

What To Do?

- Believing the problem lies with our "truster," and God can give us what we need, *is actually an act of trust in God*, which is a step in the right direction.
- This leads us to engaging with Him for the purpose of restoring our trust.
- <u>Emotional barriers are a relational trust issue</u>, which is why "trying harder" does not help very much. We cannot repair trust by an act of the will.
- Dealing with these barriers is similar to correcting problems in any relationship. We need to talk to the person with whom we are having trouble, in this case, God Himself. Thankfully, <u>God is far more committed to resolving these barriers than we can imagine</u>.
- One thing that will build trust more than anything else is getting to know <u>the goodness of God</u>, because in order to trust we need to have confidence in the other person's character.

Many Psalms are examples of people dealing with the barriers they feel.
Ps. 10 – "Where are You, God, when things go wrong?"
Ps. 51 – "I feel so much shame..."
Ps. 61 – "I'm at the end of my rope, God."
Ps. 83 – "I really need to hear from You, God."
The lesson: take our distress to God.

Ways to talk to God about these trust issues

Anger Toward God

Motivates us to **harden** our hearts or **run** from God.
"God, I need you to help me understand my pain in this broken world..."
"God, I need to know you still care about me..."

Fear of God

Motivates us to **protect** our heart or **avoid** God.
"God, I need You to help me see your true heart for me..."

Shame

Motivates us to **hide** from God.
"God, I need to know You still love me and want to be with me..."

Hopelessness

Destroys our motivation and causes us to dismiss God as irrelevant.
"God, I need to see your vision of the work You want to do in me..."

Barriers – Summary
- Everyone encounters them.
- Important to acknowledge our barriers.
  - Barriers may take precedence over other considerations.
- Barriers are God-sized problems.
  - Take everything to God.

[Video: Session 8 – Part 2]

Making Space to Engage With God

	With Myself (**solitude**)	**With Others** (community)
Appreciating	Private Worship Spiritual Reflection Affirmation	Appreciation Stories **Service to Others** **Recovery Support**
Interacting	Listening to the Word Dialogue Repentance	Encouragement Healing Prayer Forgiveness

Service to Others
Giving away life to those around us:
- Ministering to family, friends, strangers.
  - Helping, serving, and spending time with others
    (soup kitchen, respite for caregiver, Big Brother, lending a hand, etc).
- Forming our heart and mind:
  - Training to be more like Jesus and developing our desire to give life.
  - Service stirs up unresolved issues and highlights our weaknesses. God wants to heal the minister, too!
  - Giving life creates Joy! We are designed to give life.

Service is not only about what we can do for others (as important as that is).
We are actually designed to experience joy from bringing life to others.
Service also <u>makes a space</u> for revealing areas of our heart that we would not otherwise see. When those issues rise to the surface, or when we experience something other than joy from service, we have an opportunity to engage with God and receive healing. In that way, service does not turn into another form of "rowing" but actually becomes a way of re-aligning our "sail" with God.

Recovery Support

Engaging with others to address life issues.

– Addiction recovery, grief support, cancer support, survivors of abuse.

• A well-functioning recovery group can be a great avenue for God to bring us corrective experiences through others, which can then provide us with much needed experiential truth, such as:

– I am not alone; my story has value; restoration is possible.

– My struggles are not a reason for self-condemnation.

– I can come out of hiding and risk connecting to others.

• Corrective experiences can also help us to build trust, develop appropriate boundaries, and learn other relational skills.

Solitude / Retreat

Extended time alone with God can enhance most other spiritual practices.

• Anything from a couple of hours to several days.

• Zero distractions.

• Extended reflection and dialogue.

• Alternating times of intense reflection and conversational prayer with times of rest and quiet with God.

Solitude strips away:

• Distractions that keep us from paying attention to what is important.

• External props that we use to define us or give us purpose.

• Entertainment and other ways of engaging our mind.

Solitude gives to us:

• Better focus.

• A way to hold the sacred space longer. Extended time with God.

• A chance for deeper truth to emerge.

Also consider the possibility of going on a retreat with another person. Spend some time separately engaging with God, then together sharing your experiences and praying.

Solitude has been considered a classic spiritual practice for centuries. Many of the most significant, life-changing stories of experiences with God happen during times of extended prayer and reflection. While not every retreat results in dramatic encounters, there is something about extended time with God that allows for a deeper connection than we normally experience.

Spiritual Practices

Can make a significant space to engage with God, and train our heart and mind to be more aware of God's presence and care for us.

Exercise 8 – What If You Were There?[7]

1. Read the passage below.

2. Try to enter the drama as much as possible as a participant in the event. Walk through the story as if you are actually there as (1) the woman, (2) the Pharisee, (3) Jesus, or (4) one of the dinner guests. How is your experience shaped by your character's particular perspective? What would you see, hear, smell, taste, feel, touch? What would you notice? What would be memorable about this event that you would remember a week or a month later? Six months later?

3. If you are in a large group, divide up into four smaller groups and assign one of these characters to each group. After about 20 minutes, have each group report back to the larger group what they discovered about their character's experience. Try to take into consideration anything you know about the customs and expectations of Jewish culture at that time.

Luke 7: 36-50   (New King James translation)

Then one of the Pharisees asked Him to eat with him. And He went to the Pharisee's house, and sat down to eat. And behold, a woman in the city who was a sinner, when she knew that Jesus sat at the table in the Pharisee's house, brought an alabaster flask of fragrant oil, and stood at his feet behind Him weeping; and she began to wash his feet with her tears, and wiped them with the hair of her head; and she kissed his feet and anointed them with the fragrant oil. Now when the Pharisee who had invited Him saw this, he spoke to himself saying, "This Man, if He were a prophet, would know who and what manner of woman this is who is touching Him, for she is a sinner."

And Jesus answered and said to him, "Simon, I have something to say to you."

So he said, "Teacher, say it."

"There was a certain creditor who had two debtors. One owed five hundred denarii and the other fifty. And when they had nothing with which to repay, he freely forgave them both. Tell Me, therefore, which of them will love him more?"

Simon answered and said, "I suppose the one whom he forgave more."

And He said to him, "You have rightly judged." Then He turned to the woman and said to Simon, "Do you see this woman? I entered your house; you gave Me no water for My feet, but she has washed My feet with her tears and wiped them with the hair of her head. You gave Me no kiss, but this woman has not ceased to kiss My feet since the time I came in. You did not anoint My head with oil, but this woman has anointed My feet with fragrant oil. Therefore I say to you, her sins, which are many, are forgiven, for she loved much. But to whom little is forgiven, the same loves little."

Then He said to her, "Your sins are forgiven."

And those who sat at the table with Him began to say to themselves, "Who is this who even forgives sins?"

Then He said to the woman, "Your faith has saved you. Go in peace."

---

7   The idea for this exercise comes from Joel Warne in *The Intimate Journey*

(This page is for making notes on Exercise 8)

Have each group report back what they discovered about their character (4-5 minutes each).

After all four groups have reported their findings, consider the following questions:
  • How would you summarize the difference between what most people saw in the woman and what Jesus saw in her?
  • In what ways do you think God might see us differently from how we see ourselves?
  • What does this say to us about how God looks at our past? Our failures? Our worth?
  • What does all of this say about the Father's heart for us?

Session 8 Sailing Practice – Ongoing

1. Focus on the goodness of God each morning and night (Appreciating the Goodness of God).
2. Listen to the Spirit teach you about abiding in John 14-15 (Directly Interacting).

Session 8 Sailing Practice 1 – Solitude / Retreat

Get out your calendar and mark off some time for you to get alone with God.
To begin your retreat:

Select a rich passage of Scripture to reflect on, like Isaiah 55 or Psalm 84.

Ask God to help you to sense His presence.

Begin reading and writing. Whenever things slow down a bit, re-read the passage and ask God to bring the words to life for you.

Try various other spiritual practices as you feel led throughout your retreat.

Be sure to alternate between intense times of seeking God and times of quiet rest.

Here are a few suggestions for setting up your Solitude / Retreat time with God.

At a Park: Find a place in a park that is away from vehicle traffic and people. Bring a blanket or a lawn chair and something to drink, perhaps a snack. Spend 1-2 hours reading and writing. Get up and walk around once in a while as you pray.

Retreat Center: Check your area for spiritual retreat centers, and spend at least two hours there, or consider an overnight stay if they have those facilities.

At Home: Choose a time when no one else will be home. Turn off all phone ringers, turn down the answering machine volume. Pick a comfortable place to sit. Spend 1-2 hours reading and writing.

Get-Away: Rent a budget motel room near a really good park or beach, house sit for someone, pitch a tent or get a cabin in a state park, etc. If you go with a spouse or a friend, spend an hour or more at a time doing personal reflection on the same passage, then get together and talk about what God is showing you.

Session 8 Sailing Practice 2
– Inviting God to Search Our Heart for Emotional Barriers

This is based on the idea of Ps.139, "Search me, O God."

This session addressed several common emotional barriers that get in our way of connecting with God. Ask God to reveal any <u>emotional barrier</u> (anger, fear, shame, hopelessness) that may be limiting your connection with Him. He may remind you of some barrier you noticed during the presentation, He may call your attention to something you have thought about or felt in the past, or He may point out some other area of your relationship with Him that is in need of attention.

Do not try to renounce or repent of the barrier right away, rather allow God to reveal more about it.
Where did it come from? What makes it resistant to healing?
Ask Him to show you how this barrier relates to your trust of Him.
What does God want to show you or tell you so your heart can begin to change?

Additional Reading on Spiritual Practices

Dallas Willard: *The Spirit of the Disciplines: Understanding How God Changes Lives* (HarperOne: New York) 1990

Jan Johnson: *When the Soul Listens* (NavPress: Colorado Springs) 1999

Ship's Log – Session 8

Looking at the various kinds of barriers that are possible between us and God, I think I can safely say that I have experienced them all. What makes this particularly interesting to me, though, is that I grew up in a church that was deadly serious about the Bible and about being the best Christian one could be. People there would ever want to admit having barriers between them and God. Yet it was their theology itself that created some of the most difficult barriers to building a vital relationship with God.

To begin with, they taught me that God stopped talking at the end of the first century, and that all we have left of God's word to us is the Bible. Well, certainly the Bible is a life saver when it comes to knowing right from wrong and what principles we are supposed to live by. That's a lot better than being clueless. But I had lots of questions like, "How do I know what God wants me to focus on right now?" and "How do I deal with all the hurt feelings from spending Thanksgiving with my family?" I needed personal guidance, and all I had were a lot of good principles to choose from. That's not a very workable relationship from any standpoint. Not knowing that God could speak into my life put tremendous distance between God and me that should never have been there.

Even if I had known God still speaks, it might not have helped. I was also convinced that He was extremely judgmental, watching everything I did with a great deal of disgust and disappointment. Not that I was a bad person. I just felt condemned all the time for what I thought, what I did, and what I left undone. So if God were to say anything to me, I would have thought for sure He would only shame me.

If I ever got past my shame, I would have had to deal with my fear of God. Among other things, I was afraid if I ever figured out God's will for my life, it would mean doing something I dreaded. After all, I was sure God would always make us do whatever we were most resistant to doing. I was even careful not to say out loud anything I wanted, because I was sure God would then see to it that I never got it.

Those were some of the barriers presented by the bad theology I was taught. Then there were the things I learned growing up. For example, I learned never to trust anyone. Don't ever ask for help, if you can avoid it. Don't let anyone see you make a mistake. Try to look competent, even if you have no idea what you are doing. Avoid contact when possible. Don't expect much. I think you get the picture.

Needless to say, my "truster" was smashed beyond recognition. So even though I would have told you I trusted God, it was only because that's what a good Christian is supposed to say and believe. But when it came to real life, I depended on my own wits and willpower to make choices and deal with my anxieties about the world. The truth is, I didn't even know I didn't trust God until I started having conversations with Him. Up until then, my trust was rarely tested. But once I began engaging with Him and learning how to have a real relationship with Him, my busted "truster" made itself known, loud and clear.

Even now I have days when I don't want to talk to God, days when I want to be left alone, and issues that get in the way of our relationship. The good news is that I have seen enough of these to know that no matter how it feels to me, I know that God is good and that His heart is good toward me. Whatever it is that I'm dealing with, He knows what to do about it more than I do, and He wants to help me.

David Takle
Sailor Apprentice

SESSION 9 – RENEWING OUR MIND
HOW TRUTH CAN SET YOU FREE[8]

"Do not conform any longer to the pattern of this world,
but be transformed by the renewal of your mind" (Rom.12:2).

Paul tells us that renewing our mind will transform our life. But what exactly does that mean? *How* do we renew our mind? Why is it so hard to do? Is it something that God does in us? If so, what do we need to do in order to participate with Him in that?

This lesson will examine the actual process of renewing our mind, including what that really means and how it happens. We will also look at why renewing our mind makes such a big difference in how we live. Along the way we will discover why traditional "rowing" approaches to the Christian life not only fail to renew our mind, but actually make life more difficult!

Throughout this lesson we will be talking about **beliefs that we internalize from life experience**. When we use the word ***belief*** in this way, we are <u>not</u> referring to doctrines or ideas of God that we heard in church. Instead, these are the beliefs we have picked up from repeated life experience.

For example, I may say that I believe God is totally good. But when some tragedy happens to me or someone in my family, I may find myself questioning whether God's goodness extends to me, or whether He is good at all. What I *say* I "believe" or what I think I *should* believe can be very different from what I *really believe.* My gut reaction in a moment of crisis is usually more reflective of those deeply internalized beliefs than the ones I learned in Sunday School.

This internal mix of beliefs is often referred to as a head/heart split. I may intellectually accept the idea that God has forgiven me, while at the same time my whole being feels condemned by my mistakes, both past and present. All those thoughts and images that lead me to feel condemned come from internalized *beliefs* that I hold about myself.

What is interesting about internalized beliefs is that they can be quite resistant to change. If my experience tells me that getting close to other people is dangerous and I am better off alone, telling me that we are designed for relationships will probably not make much difference to me. If I try to override my belief by deliberately choosing to get close to someone, most likely I will hear a chorus of alarm bells going off in my head telling me to run the other way. The inner belief is still having its say in my life.

Of course, we can also internalize healthy beliefs. John records something along those lines when he says, "We have come to know and have believed the love which God has for us" (1Jn.4:16 NASB). John knew from personal experience that he was totally loved by God. These are the kinds of beliefs we want to internalize deeply. Replacing our doubts about God's love with this kind of knowing is what Paul calls *renewing the mind*.

So the big questions is, How do we root out these faulty beliefs we have picked up from life in this broken world and replace them with true beliefs? That is the goal of this session.

---

8   This session is taken from David Takle, *The Truth About Lies and Lies About Truth*

[Video: Session 9 – Part 1]

What Needs Renewing?

We all have distorted ideas about who we are, who God is, how life works for us, how relationships work.

"Do not be confirmed any longer to the pattern of this world, but be transformed by the renewing of your mind" (Rom.12:2).

Examples of common distorted beliefs:[9]
• You are only as good as how well you perform.
• If our marriage takes such hard work, we must not be right for each other.
• Depression, anger, and other emotional problems are a sign of weak faith.
• If I'm doing my best, then God should protect me from pain and suffering.
• God will help other people, but not me. Life should be fair.
• If I make mistakes, I am worthy of being rejected.

If these are the kinds of beliefs driving our perceptions, interpretations and responses, we would expect to have trouble living out the abundant life.

An Interactive Model – Basic View

The diagram below is a simplified model of how we interact with the world around us, whether with an event, a circumstance, or another person.

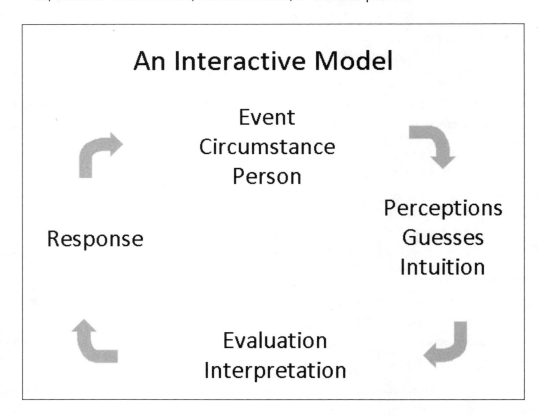

---

9   Chris Thurman, *The Lies We Believe*

- **Event:** Whatever we are dealing with – anything external to us.
- **Perception:** The raw data we collect, which may or may not be accurate.
- **Evaluation:** How we interpret the raw data.
- **Response:** Our internal reactions and external action or inaction.

In any given interaction, we gather some raw data through our five senses, sometimes filling in the blanks with our best guesses. We then interpret that information in order to understand what we are dealing with. Finally, we have some internal emotional responses and possibly external responses (verbal or physical) to that event / circumstance / person.

Only the event / circumstance / person is external to us.
The other areas: perception, evaluation, and response are processes that take place inside of us. **Examples:**

(1) Reactions to physical events like an insect buzzing around.

Regardless of what kind of insect it really is, my reaction will be completely dependent upon what kind of insect I perceive it to be and how I interpret my safety as a result of that perception.

(2) Reaction to misunderstanding and then correcting that misunderstanding.

My perception about what was said drives my interpretations and responses, regardless of whether or not I heard the other person correctly.

Basic Principles

While the above examples are very simple to resolve, they demonstrate several important principles:

- My emotions are caused by my perceptions and interpretations, not by external events.
- The more closely my perceptions and interpretations match reality, the more appropriate and effective my responses can be.
- What most needs to change to live more effectively are my own perceptions and interpretations – those things that are going on inside me.

Of course, much of the time our perceptions are reasonably accurate and our interpretations are well informed, so that the part of our mind which determines our response has good information to start with.

Our focus here is about what causes us to _malfunction_ in responding to situations where our emotions, internal impulses, or actions are not as healthy as we wish they were.

An Interactive Model – Driven by Internal Beliefs

Now let's take into consideration the influence of our internalized beliefs.

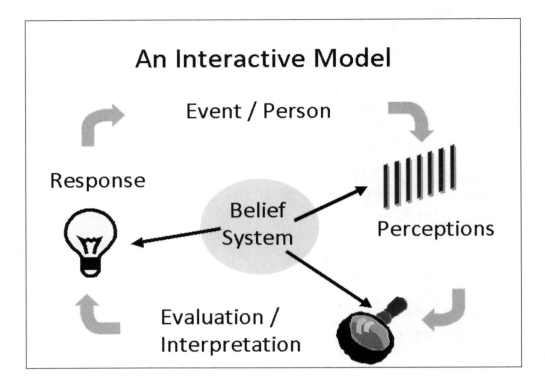

Internal Belief System: We arrive at hundreds of conclusions about life by personal experience. This system holds beliefs about what we can expect from ourselves, others, and God. It has very strong ideas about what we can hope for, who we are and how we matter, how power gets used, how life works, how God is involved, etc. Much of this system lies below the conscious level, and we are often unaware of its influence on our perceptions, interpretations and responses.

Perceptions: We filter incoming observations, so the data effectively gets altered even before we have a chance to evaluate it. Examples:

(1) I expect you to be upset or disagree with me, so I hear a challenge from you even if you do not intend it.

(2) I expect to be ignored, so I see everyone ignoring me.

(3) I do not expect God to be close, so I fail to perceive Him.

Interpretations: Our interpretations of events can vary a lot depending on our inner belief system. Examples:

(1) Your comments right now remind me of my father. He was always mean and critical, so you are trying to be mean to me.

(2) God did not meet my expectations; therefore He is not trustworthy.

(3) I need to hide my mistakes because mistakes are unacceptable.

Response: Our responses depend upon our beliefs about: (1) what might be appropriate; (2) what might be effective; (3) what might be within our ability. Examples:

(1) It's best to hide my true feelings.

(2) My attempts to deal with things are rarely effective, so why bother.

(3) Anything goes, as long as I win.

Interactive Example

Event: Someone backs into my new BMW and dents it.

My perceptions, interpretations, reactions will depend on my <u>underlying beliefs</u>.

Belief: <u>My car reflects my self-worth.</u>
> Perception:
> Interpretation:
> Response:

Belief: <u>Murphy's Law rules my life.</u> (Whatever can go wrong, will go wrong.)
> Perception:
> Interpretation:
> Response:

Belief: <u>God micro-manages everything that happens.</u>
> Perception:
> Interpretation:
> Response:

A difference in internal beliefs is one of the main reasons why two people will respond to the same kind of event very differently, or why we look back years after an event and say, "I wish I knew then what I know now!"

There is tremendous evidence to support this model.

We routinely say to ourselves, "I wish I had known then what I know now." Why? Because of the life experience we have had in the mean time. We have internalized new conclusions about what is important, how life works, and so on. As a result, we see things differently, we interpret them differently, and we react differently.

Important: *Our responses are NOT caused by other people or external events, but by our own <u>internal system</u> of seeing and interpreting the world, most of which is driven by <u>beliefs</u> that we have internalized from prior life experience.*

Our main problem, spiritually, is that the inner circle of internalized beliefs is ***full*** of mistaken ideas about life, distorted images of God and His involvement in our life, and distorted ideas about who we are.

Exercise 9A – Perceptions and Observations About Life

For each of the items below ask, **How <u>often</u> do I feel or think this way?**
Rate each one from 0 to 5 using the scale below. If a particular item seems dependent upon particular people or circumstances, feel free to make a note next to the item and give it a second rating as well.

0=never   1=rarely   2=occasionally   3=sometimes   4=often   5=most of the time

___ I am afraid of what God wants from me

___ I think God is disappointed in me

___God seems very distant from me

___ I feel angry at God about things that have happened to me

___ I have doubts about God's interest or concern for me

___ I'm better off alone than trying to get close to others

___ I have places in my life where I feel stuck and cannot seem to change

___ I feel judgmental or contemptuous toward others

___ I compare myself to others and feel as if I don't measure up

___ I seem to need everyone to like me and/or approve of me

___ There are people that I'm not sure I can ever forgive

___ I have trouble "forgiving myself" for mistakes I have made

___ I am afraid of making mistakes or failing at things I try

___ I am surprised by how negative my reaction can be to certain situations

___ I have painful regrets about choices I have made

___ I believe negative feedback more than positive

___ I worry about finances

___ I'm really hard on myself

___ Evil seems more powerful than good

There is no scoring for this survey. The purpose is to call attention to areas which may indicate the presence of underlying beliefs that God wants to change.

Forms of Deception / Darkness

Deception: Any way that our internalized beliefs are distorted or incomplete. Our understanding of life, God, and even our own identity, is terribly distorted. Deception is absolutely pervasive.

Lies	Misinformation	Mistaken Goals
Unbelief	Misinterpretation	• Self protection
Ignorance	False Assumptions	• Self importance • Winning
Confusion	Twisting the Truth	• Perfectionism
Corruption	Distortion	• Need to be right

[Video: Session 9 – Part 2]

An Interactive Model

To whatever extent the inner circle of internalized beliefs is distorted

we will find it difficult to live as God intended us to.

Consider a metaphor of trying to use a map that has been severely altered. Roads and bridges have been drawn in where there are dead ends, street names have been changed, and the index points to the wrong areas. The more dedicated we are to this map of the area, the worse things will be for us. Similarly, the more distorted out internal "map" and the more dedicated we are to it, the harder life is for us.

Deception Causes Failure

- **Garden of Eden:** Adam and Eve were deceived and lost their trust in God. That is why they ate the fruit.
- **Failure to Enter the Promised Land:** The Israelites believed the giants were too big for them. They also believed that God hated them.
- **Missed Their Own Messiah:** The Pharisees had a preconceived idea of what the Messiah would be like.
- **False Christs:** Jesus warned that being misled by false Christs will lead to disaster.
- **Entire Book of Proverbs:** Wisdom leads to life, and the lack of wisdom leads to misery, disaster, or death.

Unbelief is not a lack of belief; it is belief in the wrong things.

Belief in the wrong things leads us to failure. That is why the whole area of belief and unbelief is such a major theme in Scripture and why it is so closely tied to the issues of truth and deception.

Notes **How Do We Come to Believe Lies?**

How does that inner circle get corrupted in the first place?

Any life experience that we interpret apart from God's perspective
    is prone to distortions that we may then internalize as core beliefs.

There are many potential sources for these experiences.

- **Family:** messages about whether you matter, what you need to do in order to have value, how boys and girls matter – all the ways you are trained to view yourself. Nearly everything characterizing dysfunctional families is rooted in lies.
- **Culture:** values about individualism, materialism, sexuality; what labels you wear.
- **Life Experience:** getting sick, having an accident, getting fired, losing a friend.
- **Father of Lies:** has a vested interest in confusing and distorting everything that matters (C.S. Lewis: *Screwtape Letters*)

Examples: (1) A child who has a highly critical father may grow up thinking "I will never be good enough." (2) A boy whose mother has a lot of hatred toward men may internalize her issue as a rejection of himself. (3) Children rejected by their peers often carry tremendous self-hate or hopelessness for years.

Conclusions About Deception

- Spiritual darkness (deception) is pervasive.
- Being deceived is sufficient in and of itself to keep us in bondage.
- <u>Bad things that happen to us</u> can generate lies that keep us in bondage.
- <u>Bad things we do</u> come out of lies we believe (and create more lies).

Like the Israelites backing away from the Promised Land, we make poor choices
    because of our mistaken interpretations of life.

The disciples argued about who would be greatest in the kingdom, because they
    had internalized distorted beliefs about what greatness was.

Conclusions About Deception

*Our primary source of spiritual difficulty is the set of beliefs we have internalized
from life experience.*

- What we **do not** know (our lack of vision and understanding).
- What we **think** we know – falsely (distortions we have internalized).
- Distorted views of God, of self, and of how life works (especially relationships).

Key to Transformation

This understanding of the human problem leads us naturally to a solution.

If beliefs drive our lives ....

- Faulty beliefs create bondage and death.
- True beliefs create freedom and life.

Then replacing faulty beliefs with truth will change how we live.

We will have better perceptions, interpretations, and responses.

Good News!

We can become more free as we internalize truth!

"You will <u>know the truth</u>, and the truth will set you free" (Jn.8:32).

"Seeing that you have stripped off the old self with its practices and have clothed yourselves with the new self, which is *<u>being renewed in knowledge</u>* according to the image of its creator" (Col.3:9-10).

Not All Truth Transforms

But we encounter truth all the time without being changed!

What makes the difference? How do we internalize truth?

- So that it actually replaces our faulty beliefs.
- So that it transforms our life.

We read the Bible, hear sermons, go to conferences, read books.

Why doesn't all that truth change our internalized distortions?

Why does Christian education only take us a short way before we get stuck?

Improper Focus

This is the single most common reason we encounter truth without being changed. We think of truth as a way to focus on <u>how to respond</u>.

What we *should* do, how we *should* feel, attitudes we *ought* to have.

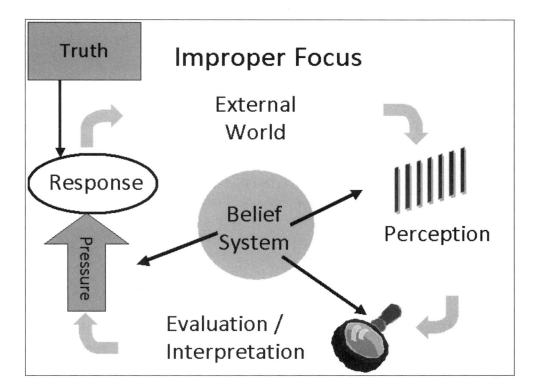

We try to force the outcome by sheer willpower, trying to override all the *pressure* that is coming from the rest of our internal system of evaluation (this is a ROWING approach to change)

This creates an internal war between the truth that we hear and the beliefs we hold from life experience. *This is what is going on when we feel a disagreement between our head and our heart.*

Example: I know I am supposed to love my neighbor. But everything inside me is offended by him, and I have nothing good to say about him.

Example: I know I should forgive this person who wronged me, and I can even force myself to say, "I forgive you." But nothing has changed inside, and I still think he owes me for what he did.

Example: I know I should not be judgmental toward others, but everything in me feels contempt toward certain people.

Focusing on Response / Action
- Looks for answers to the question "What <u>should</u> I do *?"*
- Distorts our understanding of truth.
  - Viewed primarily as information about right and wrong behavior.
  - Lots of emphasis on "obedience" and "accountability."
  - Engages the internal war with willpower.
- This approach to applying truth is an attempt to live by following Laws.
- This is trying to do the right thing without being transformed.
- Jesus called this "cleaning the outside of the cup."

Proper Focus for Truth
Allowing God to use truth as a light to illuminate and change our heart.

Truth is not so much about <u>what to do</u>, but about <u>seeing what God sees</u>.

This goes beyond simply exposing what is in our heart. Rather, God reveals to us the *significance* of what we falsely believe, the *meanings* we attach to those beliefs, and the *reality* of a far more life-giving view of those areas of life.

This is <u>renewing</u> our mind. This is aligning the sail.

Example: When the disciples argued about being the greatest, Jesus did not tell them "Stop that! Good disciples do not argue." Instead He taught them about the true nature of greatness, because if they could get that, there would be no basis for competition and disagreement among them.

Example: When asked, "Our oppressors want us to pay taxes. What should we do?" Jesus did not tell them how to respond to Rome. Instead He helped them to see <u>what</u> things belonged to <u>whom</u>. If Caesar wants his money back, so be it. You can still give God what belongs to God. Once you see the truth of this, you no longer have to fret over paying taxes imposed by the government.

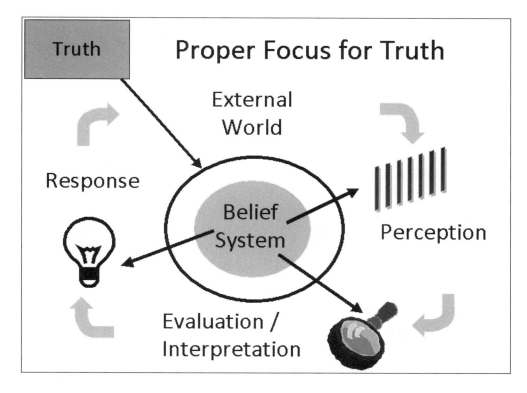

Focusing on Internal Beliefs

- Looks for answers to the questions:
    "What am I missing?"
    "How are my beliefs distorted?"
- Sees truth as God's perceptions and interpretations of our life
    (which may be very different from our own).
- Engages the internal war at the source.

This is the difference between the Law written on stone tablets (telling us what to <u>do</u>) and laws written on our heart (changing our internalized beliefs).
Every time an internal belief re-aligns with God's view, the inner war is diminished.

Renewing Our Mind

- This is something only God can do.
    – Not something we can manage by trying harder to do the right thing.
- The Holy Spirit is our Mentor and Healer.
- We can engage with the Holy Spirit to reveal what God sees that we do not.
    – Beliefs we hold in our heart that are distorted.
    – Truth we are missing that we need.
- If we truly see what God sees, it will change our heart.
- We then have a way of pursuing our healing by deliberate, intentional means.
- Instead of compliance (forcing responses) we seek renewal (changing beliefs).

This is why we need to become life-long learners in the Kingdom.

As things come up in our life that hint of inner distorted beliefs, we can seek His truth and be changed by Him so that we can become more of who He designed us to be. Difficult life experiences then become opportunities for new life, instead of tests of endurance. Trials become teachable moments, and wounds become addressable and receptive to His healing touch.

Exercise 9B – Healing Mistaken Beliefs

The goal of this exercise is to engage with God very directly and ask Him to shine His light of truth on an internalized belief that you hold.

1. Choose one item from Exercise 9A with a rating of 2 or 3 that you want to talk to God about. Make sure that it is an issue you can connect with emotionally.
2. Begin by recalling an appreciation moment. Ask God to open your heart to His presence and voice.
3. Ask God to help you remember a situation when the item you selected felt particularly true.
4. When you have a a sense of both God's involvement and the item you are considering,
     ask God <u>what He wants to reveal to you</u> about that experience:
   • If there are internalized beliefs you already hold in your heart that need healing.
   • Any perspectives of life or experience of God you are missing and need from Him.

Record your thoughts and impressions as you ponder this issue. Remember, sensing God's truth is not passive. Stay engaged, while exploring the subject and listening at the same time.

Session 9 Sailing Practice – Ongoing

1. Focus on the goodness of God each morning and night (Appreciating the Goodness of God).
2. Listen to the Spirit teach you about abiding in John 14-15 (Directly Interacting).

Session 9 Sailing Practice – Healing Mistaken Beliefs

Read the following article, *A Model for Healing Distorted Beliefs*.
Choose another item from Exercise 9A that has a rating of 2 or 3.
Make sure that it is an issue you can connect with emotionally.
  • Ask God to open your heart to His presence and your mind to His voice.
  • Ask God to help you remember a situation when this item felt particularly true.
  • When you have a sense of both God's involvement and the thing you are considering,
    ask God what He wants to reveal to you about that experience.
      • What you already hold in your heart that needs healing.
      • Whatever it is that you are missing and need from Him.
Record your thoughts and impressions throughout this time.

Additional Reading on Renewing Our Mind

David Takle: *The Truth About Lies And Lies About Truth* (Shepherd's House: Pasadena) 2008
Gary Smalley: *Change Your Heart, Change Your Life: How Changing What You Believe Will Give You the Great Life You've Always Wanted* (Thomas Nelson: Nashville) 2008
Jim Wilder, Chris Coursey: *Share Immanuel* (Shepherd's House: Pasadena) 2010

A Model for Restoration of Distorted Beliefs

Through a lot of experience, Christian counselors and ministers who assist others with healing prayer have found a fairly effective way of helping people engage with God to permanently alter the underlying beliefs that cause so much pain and faulty living. The model for prayer outlined below is an adaptation of several of these approaches.[10] Please bear in mind that this is a very brief description of this kind of prayer. The reader is encouraged to check out additional sources on renewing our mind for a more in-depth discussion of inner healing prayer, especially any materials based on the "Share Immanuel" lifestyle.

1. Find a place of appreciation and ask Jesus to open your heart to His presence. It may be helpful to remember a time when you were keenly aware of His presence and ask God to stir up your memory of that time. When you begin to have a sense of the presence of God, ask Him to come closer and reveal Himself to you even more. (If you have difficulty sensing His presence, ask Him to reveal whatever might be in the way. This then becomes the issue to take to step 3.)

2. Discern what needs to be addressed. If you have a specific issue that you want healing for, ask God if this is the time and place for that. Otherwise, ask God if He has something else that He would like to talk about.

3. Once you have named the issue to be addressed, identify the emotions that are associated with it. Describe any reactions, beliefs and intentions that go with the experience and/or distress, and any means by which the issue may get triggered in your life.

4. Ask Jesus to help you bring the issue into focus, using your memory of either an actual event or the people involved. Generally speaking, as long as you can stay connected with God, the more you are able to re-experience the distressing emotions related to this issue, the more open you will be to change. If you have identified a faulty belief that is involved, the more "true" that it feels to you, the more deeply the real truth will be able to penetrate.

5. Check to make sure you are still connected to God as you talk to Him about this issue. If the emotions become overwhelming, be sure to back off and ask God for help in seeing Him first and foremost.

6. Ask God what He wants you to know about this issue and be open to whatever He might say or do at that point. He may reveal truth in the form of words or images, or He may reveal His heart toward you, assure you that you are not alone, or whatever it is you need in that moment. If you are not receiving anything, make sure you can see Him or sense His presence, and ask Him questions about the issue that will help to expose any underlying fears and beliefs.

7. After you have received something that you believe is from God, check for peace and rest in the event. If you have experienced His peace, the process is probably done. If the emotion has simply changed, say from shame to sadness, then there may be more that needs to be addressed. Start over and see what else needs God's touch.

---

10 This model draws from several approaches to engaging with God for healing our internal beliefs about life. See the following authors: Koepcke, et.al.; Lehman; Wilder-Coursey; Takle.

8. Give thanks for the healing that has occurred.

The most important factor in all of this is staying connected with God. If at any point it becomes difficult to sense the presence of God, then everything else becomes secondary to finding out what is preventing us from sensing His presence. Sometimes all that is needed is to notice that we have lost track of God and seek Him out again. Sometimes we will discover one or more obstacles in the way of perceiving His presence, such as fear of God, fear of pain, anger at God, vows we have made related to the issue or in regard to God, disbelief about healing or about God, and so on. These obstacles then become the issues that need to be addressed, taking them back to God just as the original issue was taken to God, asking Him how He wants to address these things.

For example, if you discover that you are angry with God for not preventing a certain event from happening, then it is probably more important to deal with God about your anger than it is to seek healing in regard to that event. Or if you find that you do not believe He wants to heal you, tell Him what you feel and ask Him what you need to know about your disbelief. In any case, whenever anything gets in the way of your relationship and receptivity to God, your primary concern is to address those things with God.

Looking back at the entire process, notice the level of participation that is required by both yourself and God. Seeking out the best evidence for a faulty belief can mean recalling a very painful event where the belief became anchored in your memory. You must be willing and able to hold significant levels of discomfort while remaining open to the voice of God.

It is often helpful to have another person present with you and interceding for you (even out loud, occasionally) while you engage with God for healing. But it is generally better for your intercessor to be patient as you wrestle with God, and not attempt to provide the truth that he or she thinks you need. (There is a time and place to receive wisdom from others. But in inner healing prayer, it is best to receive from God directly – His words have the power of life in them.)

There are often multiple distortions embedded in single events, and there can be multiple events woven together to arrive at one or more faulty beliefs. Dealing with these complications and listening to God while in distress is a learned process for both the minister and the one being ministered to. That is why it is important to take into account all of the distress surrounding particular events, and why we should not abandon this process when we run into a few dead ends. Patience and persistence are valuable assets in any aspect of spiritual formation, and especially when addressing painful wounds.

Learning to engage with God to reinterpret your life experiences from His point of view is one of the most exciting and life-giving experiences we can have. We discover more of God's heart for us and find a freedom we never thought possible. May God richly bless your pursuit of His gifts.

For more information on inner healing, see the resources in the appendix and on the following websites:
www.lifemodel.org
www.kclehman.com
www.TruthAboutLies.info
www.KingdomFormation.org

Ship's Log – Session 9

Like most families, the one I grew up in had its share of problems. From the outside looking in, it looked pretty good. I'm even quite grateful for what we had. There were always great food, nice clothes, a car in the driveway, and more toys that we really knew what to do with. It was a nice middle-class family.

But on the inside, things were not always so tidy. By the time I had reached sixth grade, there were seven of us. I had an older brother and sister, fairly close in age, and a younger brother and sister who were quite far apart in age. I was completely miserable most of the time and tried to stay away from everyone in the house as much as possible. The emotional atmosphere was toxic at best. While there had never been any outward signs of affection, which had taken its own toll, the constant attacks and counter attacks between family members were more than I could bear. One of my siblings, in particular, I was certain stayed awake nights dreaming up new ways to make life more painful than it already was.

Among other things, there existed a pervasive sense of contempt for nearly everyone and everything outside the home – the crazy world "out there" that we all had to deal with. Every discomfort, every disappointment was due to some horrible person who ought to know better. But that contemptuous weapon could just as easily be turned on someone inside the house, whenever the situation presented itself. Actually, almost anything I said or did could become a target. It was as if humiliation of others were some kind of sport used for entertainment purposes. I found it intolerable.

Needless to say, I got away as soon as I could after high school. But for years I kept going "home" for major holidays because that was what was expected. As often as not, the reunions ended in fights, name calling, and other forms of abuse, because nothing ever got resolved. And over the years my resentment and anger toward the emotional violence grew into hatred and bitterness that ate away at my soul.

Now being a "good Christian," I tried everything I could to deal with my stuff. I repented of my hate. I renounced my bitterness. I wrote letters to family members. I met with them one-on-one. Whatever any Christian leader has ever said you are supposed to do in order to honor your family, I tried. And after many years of doing everything I could think of, I still hated them. The only good thing that came out of all that effort was that I realized it mostly came down to three people in the family. They were the ones I held responsible for the demise of what little family life we did have, and I could not stop hating them for the devastation they left behind them in their wake.

Finally, I gave up on my own efforts to change my heart and cried out to God for healing. What He gave me was a short video in my mind of my family members out in about twelve feet of water, all trying desperately to stay afloat so they could breathe. Each one would grab the closest person and push them under to get a little higher and gasp for air. Then someone else would grab that person and do the same thing. As I watched this gasping mass of people thrashing about, a thought occurred to me that I had never had before. *"They're not being mean ... they're desperate."* It broke my heart. For the first time in decades, I could feel compassion instead of hate for these people I did not like, and my heart toward them has never been the same. Only God knew what I needed. Only God could do what was necessary to change my heart. When it comes to the hard things in life, trying harder rarely works. We need God.

David Takle
Sailor Apprentice

SESSION 10 – HEALING OUR IDENTITY AND SELF-REJECTION
RESTORING OUR TRUE IDENTITY

This session addresses head-on one of the most wide-spread, pernicious problems that people face – self-rejection and self-hate. Most of us have thought at one time or another, "If you knew me better, you probably would not like me." The fact that one is a Christian usually does very little to alleviate the severity of this painful little secret.

In fact, there are some ways in which the current climate in the Western Christian world makes this problem even worse. First, since a very common view of the Christian life is that we are being tested to see if we can live up to God's expectations, many people feel like they are failing at what they think they should be doing. The more they learn about the Christian life, the more they feel like a failure.

Second, there are those who believe Christians are nothing more than sinners who have been granted a pardon. This shallow form of the gospel gives us no reason to hope for any significant restoration, thus effectively removing the keys to the Kingdom. It makes sense to reject ourselves because we are still sin-filled, sinful people.

Third, there are some who mistake self-abasement for true spiritual humility, and believe that unless you more or less hate yourself you are in grave danger of being prideful. Self-hate is contrasted with being self-centered, as if those were the only two options open to us. Since it is easy to show that Christians should not be self-absorbed, the only reasonable alternative left to us in this scenario is self-rejection. But this is really a false dichotomy.

Contrary to what some might think, self-hate is *not* a Christian virtue. It comes easily enough to people everywhere, Christian or not. Self-hate is truly a legacy of our broken world, and God does not want us to be held captive all our life by such an evil force. Instead, He offers us healing and restoration of our broken identity, much like what the father offered his prodigal son in the parable (Lk.15).

Self-hate comes in a great many forms and is not always easily identified. Much of what appears to be pride or arrogance is often a cover for feelings of inadequacy, a way of compensating or trying to prove to ourselves that we are not as bad as we fear we might be. Often feelings of self-hate get pushed so far down in our consciousness that we are no longer aware of them. But as we saw in the last session, those internalized beliefs will still drive our life whether we know about them or not.

Even if we are fortunate enough to have a reasonably well-balanced view of ourselves, there are still ways in which life in this world can erode and distort various elements of our identity. And every distortion makes it harder to live as God intended. So we need to learn how to engage with God to restore our true identity.

This session will demonstrate that the sources and consequences of self-hate are truly evil in nature, and something that God wants to deliver us from. We will also make good use of the resources studied so far, to show how we can find healing in these areas.

[Video: Session 10 – Part 1]

Self-Hate / Self-Rejection
- What does it looks like?
- How does it affect our lives?
- What are the real causes?
- How do we address it?

Self-hate is a highly toxic form of self-loathing and disgust that rejects our own life or self as having value.

What Self-Hate Looks Like – Direct Forms
- Self-derision / self-vindictive criticism.
    - I can't seem to do anything right.
    - I hate myself when I mess up / procrastinate / say the wrong thing.
    - No matter what I do, I don't matter.
    - The "Charlie Brown" syndrome.
- Minimizing of assets and blessings.
    - I know it won't last.
    - I'm just waiting for the other shoe to drop.
    - Compliments make me feel really uncomfortable ("it was nothing").
- Some forms of depression.
    - May be a direct *result* of self-hate.
    - Depression can also be a *cause* for self-hate.
    - Note: depression can be caused by many other things as well.
- Some addictions.
    - Alcohol, drugs, food, and even adrenaline-producing experiences can be used to medicate feelings of self-rejection.
    - These things can also deliver "well-deserved" punishment as needed.
- Fear in regard to how God sees me.
    - Feelings of shame and being judged.
    - If I am disappointed in me, then God must be disappointed, too.

What Self-Hate Looks Like – Indirect Forms
- Anxious perfectionism. (What if I overlook something?)
- Fear of making mistakes.
    - My performance defines me.
- Illusions of grandeur.
    - Used as a way to escape from feelings of inferiority.
- Over-achieving, when used as a way of compensating.
    - Feeling the need to prove we are better than what others say about us.
- Perpetual state of discontentment with life.
    - If only I had … the perfect love / family / job.
    - Rejecting the life I now have, and waiting for life to "happen" for me.

How Self-Hate Affects Us

- Adds to our distorted images of God.
  - God does not like me. He wants to make life difficult for me.
- Generates disbelief / weak faith.
  - God will not help me. He might help others, but not me.
  - My issues will never be healed. I will never have what I need.
- Causes difficulty with receiving.
  - Feel as if I do not deserve anything. Feel guilt or shame when receiving.
  - Do not believe anything good I have will last.
- Causes us to excluding ourselves from belonging.
  - Tendency to withdraw and assume no one will want to be around me.
- Damages relationships.
  - My low expectation of other people's responses to me will limit my investment in relationships. Also, to whatever extent I feel unlovable, I will notice that you do not love me well enough.

Where Self-Hate Comes From

Early childhood wounding.

- B-Type injuries are <u>bad</u> things that should not have happened.
  - Getting shamed for normal childhood behavior.
  - Constant criticism.
  - Personal boundaries violated (giving the message, "I am junk").
- A-Type injuries are due to the <u>absence</u> of good things that you need.
  - Lack of adequate bonding; never getting hugged.
  - Little or no help in learning relational skills.
  - Being ostracized.

Where Self-Hate Comes From

Personal failures that we interpret as evidence of deficiencies.

- Failed relationships / rejection.
- Failed performance / bankruptcy / loss of Job.

Where Self-Hate Comes From

Poor theology (see notes at start of chapter).

- "Miserable sinner" Christianity.
  - False understanding of humility as self-abasement.
  - Weak gospel that pardons us but leaves us as sinners.
- Severe parenting styles that claim to be "Christian."
  - Tries to eradicate sin in children through strictness and punishment.
  - Treats children like small adults, bypassing their developmental needs.
  - Children tend to see themselves through their parents' eyes, and will easily internalize whatever meanings are implicit in the parents' treatment of them.

Exercise 10A – A Survey of Self-Hate / Self-Rejection Symptoms

For each of the items below ask, **How <u>often</u> do I feel or think this way, or act like this?**

0=never   1=rarely   2=occasionally   3=sometimes   4=often   5=most of the time

___ I'm really hard on myself about mistakes or oversights

___ I don't like who I am, who I have become

___ I have thoughts of self-destructive actions

___ I despair over my feelings of powerlessness

___ I felt unloved / unwanted by my parents in ways that have not been healed

___ I can allow others grace in ways that I will not allow for myself

___ I think I have an inner saboteur who tries to ruin my life

___ I feel shame or fear when receiving (gifts, help, compliments, comfort)

___ I believe negative feedback more than positive

___ I think that if you knew me better, you wouldn't like me

___ I have been cheated out of having the spouse or income or [whatever] I needed to have

___ I compare myself to others and feel inferior in some important aspects

___ I have very little self-worth   ___ I feel like I can't do anything right

___ I reject compliments   ___ I assume that people will reject me

___ I think God disapproves of me   ___ I am a perfectionist

___ I hide behind a rather strong facade   ___ I wish I had never been born

There is no scoring for this survey. The purpose is to call attention to areas which may indicate the presence of underlying beliefs that God wants to change.

[Video: Session 10 – Part 2]   Notes

How Do I See Myself?

How most people see themselves: I am the sum total of my:

Thoughts + Values + Prior choices + Experiences + Opinions of others.

- Includes the good stuff.
  - Good choices I have made and good things that have happened to me.
  - Talents and achievements.
- Includes the bad stuff.
  - Bad things that happened to me, various kinds of losses.
  - Things I regret doing or not doing.
  - My failures and my disappointment in myself.

When the bad stuff seems like too much, this assessment can be overwhelming.

This can feel so true some might think, "How could this *not* be my identity?"

How Does God See Me?

- My future hope.
  - How God intends to form me and restore me in this life.
  - God knows how this story ends and what I am destined for.
- My past.
  - Things done to me that He wants to heal.
  - Things I have done that He has forgiven.
  - Ways I've been malformed that He will transform to be more like Him.
- My present true self.
  - I am one in whom God is at work ... a work in progress.

What About All the "Stuff"?

My flaws do not say who I am as much as they say how much I need God.

- My true identity is the person that God created me to be.
  - Evidence of this is my longing to be more like Him.
  - We need to distinguish between our true heart and our malfunctions.

  "We ourselves, who have the firstfruits of the Spirit, groan inwardly as we wait eagerly for our adoption" (Rom.8:23).

- The negative aspects of my character are those parts which have not yet come into alignment with my true identity.

  "You have put on the new self, which is being renewed in knowledge" (Col.3:9-10).

The Christian life is not a test to see how well we do. It is a relationship with a God who knows how to heal us and make us whole.

God Says I Am ...

- A new creation (2Cor.5:17).
- His child (Jn.1:12) (1Jn.3:1).
- Complete in Christ (Col.2:9-10).
- A member of Christ's body (1Cor.12:27).
- God's temple (1Cor.3:16).
- God's workmanship (Eph.2:10).
- A light in the world (Mt.5:14).
- A holy and royal priest (1Pet.2:5,9).
- A minister of reconciliation (2Cor.5:17-21).

People try to tell us who we are. We even make our own evaluation about who we are. But God is the only one who is qualified to say who we really are.

God's Intentions Toward Me

- He does not condemn me (Rom.8:1).
- He planned to rescue me (Eph.1:3-5).
- He lavishes His grace on me (Eph.1:7-8).
- He loves me even when I sin (Rom.5:8).
- He wants to live with me and in me (Jn.14:16-23).

Who am I?

I am a person in relationship with God, and He knows what I need for life.
We can only know who we really are in the context of our relationship to God. He is the only one who knows us well enough and holds us in His heart with enough love to have the right to say who we really are.

Distorted Sense of Self

Any experience in which you are not seen through the eyes of heaven
    will distort your sense of who you really are.
The more you see yourself as God sees you, the less self-hate is possible.

Key Truth

- My true self is the person that God created me to be.
- *Self-hate is always rooted in distorted perceptions* of who we are
    and what we do not yet know about the Father's love.
- We need to ask God to give us His view of who we really are
    and to help us experience His love.

Self-hate is a lie of Satan to get you to become your own worst enemy. Even when your self-hate feels true, it is rooted in distorted beliefs about who you are, and how you matter.
God wants you to be free of self-rejection, self-loathing, and self-condemnation.

Exercise 10B – Healing From Distorted Self Images

Choose an item from Exercise 10A that has a rating of 2 or 3 that you want to talk to God about.

1. Recall an appreciation moment. Ask God to open your heart to His presence and voice.

2. Ask God to help you remember where you first learned to believe this about yourself.

3. When you have a sense of both God's presence and the thing you are considering, ask God what He wants to reveal to you about that belief or perception.

   • What you already hold in your heart that needs healing.

   • Whatever it is that you are missing and need from Him.

Record your thoughts and impressions throughout this time.

Session 10 Sailing Practice – Ongoing

1. Focus on the goodness of God each morning and night (Appreciating the Goodness of God).
2. Listen to the Spirit teach you about abiding in John 14-15 (Directly Interacting).

Session 10 Sailing Practice – Healing Our Self-Image

1. Read the *Additional Information on A-Type and B-Type Injuries* at the end of this chapter.
2. Re-read the *Healing Model* From Session 9.
3. Read the *Prayer for Healing our Identity* on the next page.
4. Chose another item from the survey and repeat exercise 10B.

Additional Reading on Freedom from Self-Hate

David Benner: *The Gift of Being Yourself: The Sacred Call to Self-Discovery* (IVP Books: Downers Grove, IL) 2008

Theodore Rubin: *Compassion and Self-Hate: An Alternative to Despair* (Touchstone: New York) 1998. (His description and analysis of self-hate are superb, though being a non-Christian author, his solutions are more self-help.)

Prayer for Healing Our Identity

Lord God,

I confess to you now that over the years I have taken into my mind and heart many harmful beliefs about who I am, and many doubts about whether I could ever be free to become the person you created me to be. Some of these lies were given to me through the words and actions of others, and some of them I came to believe by my own misinterpretation of life.

But I know that these things are an attack on the person you created me to be, an attack upon the very soul that you have died to redeem and re-create in your own image. My heart is to be your servant, to submit to you and the things you want for me, and to become the person you created me to be. I open my heart and mind to your Spirit to renew my vision of how you see me. I pray that in the days to come you will purge me of all vestiges of self-hate and self-condemnation, that you will fill me with the truth of who I am, that more and more I may see myself through your eyes, and receive the grace of <u>living without condemnation</u> in the light of your love.

I receive with a grateful heart the identity you have given me. I ask that you help me to put it on and to live it out all the days of my life. I pray that I might honor your gift to me, and run to you whenever the enemy tries to come against the truth of who you are, how much you love me, or who you have made me to be.

I praise and thank you for your work in me to deliver me from a life of spiritual death and self-hate. Seal this truth, I pray, deep within my heart, and help me to remember always the beautiful life that you have given me.

In Jesus' name,
Amen.

Additional Information on A-Type and B-Type Injuries [11]

Life events that injure our souls can generally be divided into two types of wounds. A-type injuries are the *absence* of good things that we need but do not get. B-type injuries are the *bad* things that happen to us that in a perfect world would not happen. Sometimes these are referred to as *intrusions* (B-type injuries) and *deprivations* (A-type injuries). Injuries can be further divided into various categories based on the general nature of the intrusion or deprivation. Here are some examples of the major categories:

- Emotional Injury
    - A-type: lack of love or the loss of a primary caregiver
    - B-type: being terrified or unnecessarily shamed

- Physical Injury
    - A-type: malnutrition or lack of loving physical touch
    - B-type: getting beaten

- Spiritual Injury
    - A-type: lack of spiritual direction
    - B-type: being told God is disgusted with you

- Sexual Injury
    - A-type: not being taught boundaries or foundational sexual values
    - B-type: sexual assault of any kind (verbal, physical)

- Psychological Injury
    - A-type: silent treatment used for punishment; consistent favoritism shown to siblings
    - B-type: parentification of child; child required to meet needs of parents

- Developmental Injury (see also Chapter 12)
    - A-type: no help for learning an infant-level or child-level skill
    - B-type: being expected to meet adult-level expectations too soon

Notice that since B-type injuries are the result of *actual events*, they are easier to remember. On the other hand, A-type injuries are *things that are missing* from our life, so there is nothing to remember. They leave a vacuum where something good should have been. As a result, it is much harder to identify and name our A-type injuries and often harder to get healing for them as well. A-type injuries not only require God's healing perspective, but also require help from other people to give us what we missed during our development.

---

11 A more complete description of A and B type injuries can be found in *The Life Model* by Friesen, et.al.

Ship's Log – Session 10

Most of my life up until about age 55, I was burdened with incredible self-hate and self-doubt. Interestingly, I rarely saw this for what it really was. For example, I was usually keenly aware that I did not fit in well at parties and other group gatherings. But I usually thought it was because no one there was very interesting, which kept me from noticing that no one was very interested in talking to me. Yet I felt left out, and I internalized a sense of being socially deficient in some way. It was not until my thirties that it finally broke through and I consciously entertained the thought, "No one wants to be around me." Only then could I look back on my life and see I had always felt rejected by peers, family, and almost everyone else, and I hated myself for not being able to find my place.

Another way this self-hate crept up on me was my overall sense of powerlessness. It seemed as if whenever I wanted something that conflicted with what someone else wanted, I was the one who always gave in and accommodated. For a long time, I told myself it was just easier than arguing. But eventually it dawned on me that no matter what I did or wanted, I seemed to have very little control over my own life. I had long since given up on ever getting what I wanted, and I hated myself for having no voice and for being so powerless.

Much of the time my self hate was out of sight and outside of my own awareness. But every once in a while it would show up in ways that were shocking even to me. Sometimes I would explode in a fit of rage at an inanimate object that refused to bend to my wishes, like a bolt that would not loosen or a computer program that would freeze up and destroy an hour's work. These little failures seemed to mock me and highlight my inability to impact my world, and my rage at my own incompetence would often surprise me and completely overwhelm me.

In late 2006 my self-hate began to surface more intensely than ever before, and I felt as if I had no choice but to get to the bottom of it all. I spent the better part of three days wrestling with God and digging into my deepest beliefs about who I was and whether I mattered. Then suddenly, I had the sensation of a house of cards collapsing all around me. I did not have the words yet, but I knew in my soul that my self-hate had no real substance to it at all. It was all built on a pack of lies – smoke and mirrors, without a shred of truth to any of it. All I could say was, "That's not me at all! That's not who I am!"

The revelation was so startling, I nearly fell off the couch I was sitting on. I did not know whether to laugh or cry, and I remember doing a lot of both. The clarity with which I saw myself and my life story was so amazing I could hardly believe it was true. All of the things I had believed about myself were in fact terribly flawed interpretations of my life, my worth, and my self. God saw all the same details I saw (and more), but He told the story so differently, with such different interpretations and meanings, that *it became a story of redemption instead of condemnation*. It felt as if a ton of dead weight lifted from my soul. Instead of God disapproving of me, I saw Him smile and felt Him hold me in His heart. My God loved me, dearly, and *I knew* that I knew He did. His love for me was all that mattered. *He* gives me my value. *He* tells my story. No one else can tell me who I am, not even me. And I have never been the same since that day.

David Takle
Sailor Apprentice

SESSION 11 – DISARMING OUR FEAR AND ANXIETY
RESTORING OUR TRUST IN GOD

Some fears are a healthy, God-given response to danger, and to ignore them would be self-destructive. That kind of fear is a gift we gladly receive, because it helps us stay safe and avoid unnecessary risks.

But there are also many forms of fear that are *not* helpful and instead are actually self-defeating. For example, if I am afraid to get the surgery I need, I can end up with problems that are much worse than whatever it is I fear. If I am too afraid to talk with you so we can repair a rupture between us, then I may withdraw or write off our relationship even though restoration would have been possible. Or if I am afraid of making a mistake or appearing foolish, I may avoid trying new things or extending myself in ways that would be good for me.

Unfortunately, people often follow their fears even when it would be in their best interest not to. They believe their fear and assume there must be something dangerous "out there" which they need to avoid. If another person seems scary, then he or she must really be dangerous. If a new situation raises a lot of anxiety, there must be something wrong with that situation. People may or may not be aware of their own fear, but it becomes a major factor in how they respond. For example, after a person has experienced the painful loss of a significant relationship, they may develop a fear of intimacy and become very self-protective and avoid any close relationships at all. But their real need may be a life-giving relationship that is safe enough for them to experience the joy they are missing. As long as they resist getting close to anyone (including God), they will probably be unable to receive what they need in order to move on.

Fear can also cause us to become defensive when something better is called for. It can take away our voice when we need to speak at an opportune moment. Fear can make us cave in to peer pressure. It can even keep us from opening up to God or getting close to Him. In fact, we probably would not be able to list all the ways our lives have been made poorer because we listened to fear and did not deal with it very effectively.

Jesus tells us we do not need to worry or be anxious. But to many of us, that sounds like wishful thinking. Fear is not an emotion we choose to have. We just have it. And in those moments when we are afraid, the danger feels incredibly real – whether it is concern over finances or stage fright or what people will say about something we forgot to do.

Going back to Session 9, we need to see how these toxic forms of anxiety are <u>responses</u> which arise not from external events around us, but from our own perceptions and interpretations that are driven by our internal beliefs. It is not the person or circumstance that is causing us to be afraid, but rather our own internal (perhaps even subconscious) interpretation of what we are dealing with. Once we see the wisdom of this, a whole new way of dealing with our fear becomes possible. This lesson is about how to identify our fears, and how to address them in ways that offer hope for healing and a higher sense of peace in our life.

[Video: Session 11 – Part 1]

The Many Faces of Fear

God designed us with healthy fear to keep us safe. But there are also toxic forms. We use a lot of terms to describe the kinds of fear we have. Often we are not aware of our fear, precisely because we have become good at avoiding it.

Phobia	Distrust	Apprehension
Stress	Dread	Trepidation
Unsafe	Terror	Foreboding
Panic	Unease	Intimidation
Anxiety	Worry	Fright

- Phobia – a visceral reaction below the conscious level, often seems irrational.
- Foreboding – expecting something to go terribly wrong.
- Dread – combination of fear, anger, shame, sadness, and hopeless despair.
- Stress – a term used in the business world to talk about our fear of things going wrong or not getting things done in time.

Things We Fear

Mostly we fear what we might feel, especially feeling overwhelmed.

Failure	Loss of image	Loss of control
Success	Physical pain	Needs not getting met
God	Other people	Legitimate suffering
Imperfection (Making mistakes)	Intimacy, Rejection	Strong emotions: anger, shame, grief, hopeless despair

- Imperfection: Because flaws and mistakes mean that I'm defective.
- Success: It may feel safer to think that the obstacles are insurmountable.
  – I don't know who I am except as a failure.
  – Expectations will go up; then I could really fail!
- Legitimate suffering (especially significant).
  – Short term discomfort for long-term benefit.
  – Examples: surgery / moms letting kids grow up / going against peer pressure / making changes / asking for what we need / trying new things / repairing ruptures.
  – Avoiding legitimate suffering is one of the most common ways in which fear can be self-defeating. If we give in to our fear, we may seriously hurt ourselves or others in ways that we cannot see.

Ways We Are Afraid of God
- Afraid of getting too close or too far away.
- Afraid of what He thinks of me.
- Afraid of what He might do to me.
- Afraid of His will for my life.
  - Not knowing what it is (being out of God's will).
  - Finding out what it is (it might be something too hard).

How would these fears impact our relationship to God?
It is very hard to have a relationship with God when we do not trust His heart for us, how He regards us, or what His intentions are for our life.

[Video Session 11 – Part 2]

Discerning Our Fears
Fear does not always mean we need to protect ourselves from something.
- Emotions are <u>not</u> so much a reflection of external reality as much as they are an indicator of what we believe about life (Session 9).
- <u>Healthy fear</u> is designed to keep us safe (fear of falling, etc).
- <u>Toxic fear</u> drives us to seek a false kind of safety that may be a bigger problem than what we are afraid of.
  - If we fear the pain of trying new things, we may avoid change.
  - If we fear bad experiences in relationship, we may avoid intimacy.
  - If we are afraid of shame, we may be unable to tolerate self-examination.
- Toxic fear can also cause confusion, mess with our discernment, interfere with our relationships, or keep us from growing (to name a few things).

Fear Can Be a Signal
- Fear of God.
  - Signals a distorted view of God's character.
- Fear of failure, exposure, or shame.
  - Signals distorted sense of self, or how we matter.
- Anxiety about relating to others.
  - May signal mistaken beliefs about self or personal value.
  - May signal lack of trust that God is bigger than our hurts.
  - May signal lack of maturity in regard to relational skills.

These are all signals that we need some healing,
    not necessarily of real danger that requires us to protect ourselves.
If we can learn to see fear as a signal for deeper issues that need to be addressed,
    our moments of anxiety can become doorways to healing.

Notes

Exercise 11A – Naming Our Fears

The items below are things people commonly find fearful, and ways we might describe those fears. Using a scale of 0 to 5, rates the items below according to how strongly you feel fear in regard to each person or thing. Feel free to qualify any of the items, if necessary.

0 = not at all   1 = very minor   2 = somewhat   3 = moderate   4 = strong   5 = extreme

---

Ways We Describe Our Fears

Walking on eggshells	Intimidation	Unease
Unsafe	Foreboding	Anxiety
Distrust	Terror	Dread
Apprehension	Panic	Scary

People, Things, Circumstances

___My boss	___Exposure	___My own anger
___My spouse	___Failure	___Another person's anger
___My parents	___Success	___Shame
___A brother or sister	___Intimacy	___Poor health / Getting sick
___Some other relative	___God's view of me	___Death
___Rejection by others	___God's will for me	___Finances
___Work responsibilities	___Loss of control	___Wasting my life
___Family responsibilities	___Needs not being met	___Making mistakes
___Abandonment	___Physical pain	___My own inner impulses

There is no scoring for this survey. The purpose is to call attention to areas which may indicate the presence of underlying beliefs that God wants to change.

Different Kinds of "Safe"
- Controlling.
  - Trying to keep things from going wrong.
  - Attempting to avoid pain (often avoiding a false sense of shame).
- Restorative.
  - Knowing that God can restore my heart no matter what goes wrong.
  - Sometimes God will even restore my situation (an extra gift).
  - Ruptures in relationships can be repaired.
  - We can recover from hurt or loss.
- Relational.
  - Knowing who I want to be with when I am afraid.
  - Being with God as I go through life.

Controlling view of safety tries to avoid pain through controlling the environment and people around us. But in truth we have very limited control over life.

Restorative view says, "No matter what goes wrong, God can bring something good out of it or do something good in me in spite of it." That's why the Bible says so much about restoration, resurrection and the new creation.

Relational view says, "No matter what happens, God is with me."

We need to learn how to live in a broken world where things *will* go wrong.

Suffering well means learning how to stay ourselves and stay connected to God and others while suffering, rather than lashing out or getting stuck in distress.

We need both restorative and relational views of what it means to be safe in order to suffer well and trust God in the process.

Security

Security is not the absence of danger, it is the presence of God no matter what the danger (source unknown). Removing danger is not the only way to be secure.

Fear is a Trust Issue

- Fear is the opposite of trust.
- Who do I want to be with when I am afraid?

  "When I am afraid I will trust in you" (Ps.56:3).

  "The Lord is my light and my salvation; whom shall I fear? The Lord is the stronghold of my life; of whom shall I be afraid?" (Ps.27:1).

- If our real fear problem were only because the world around us is unsafe and unpredictable, then we would have to live in fear until we go to heaven.
- The truth is that toxic fear is due to our weak or broken "truster."

Notes

Rebuilding Trust

How do we build the trust we need in order to not be afraid?

- Healing old wounds.
  - Allowing God to minister to our trust-breaking experiences.
  - <u>Restorative</u> kind of safe.
- Building new trust.
  - The more we know and experience the goodness of God the more we will trust Him.
  - <u>Relational</u> kind of safe.

One of the most important goals of spiritual development is coming to a place of complete trust in God. This includes both a trust in His goodness, due to His very nature, as well as trust in His goodness toward us.

Do not underestimate either:

- The extent to which we doubt the goodness of God.
- The value of getting close enough to experience His goodness.

Redefining Goals

When I am afraid ...

- Instead of asking:
  - How do I avoid pain? (motivated by fear).
  - How do I make my world safe? (false goal).
  - How do I get away? (geographical cure).
  - What is the path of least resistance?

  These are all ways of seeking <u>control</u>.

- Asking better questions:
  - Do I know the true meaning of my fear?
  - Is this a signal that I need more healing?
  - Is this a teachable moment?
  - How does God see what I am going through right now?

  These are ways of seeking <u>restorative</u> safety.

  - Who do I want to be with when I am afraid?
  - Can I find God right now?
  - Do I know that God is with me?
  - Are there people who God is bringing alongside me?
  - What do I need to do in order to receive His peace?
  - Where is my trust?

  These are forms of <u>relational</u> safety.

Instead of trying to control things around us, what if we engage with God so He can <u>change us</u> so we are less afraid?

Exercise 11B – Asking God About Our Fear

1. Choose an item on the survey sheet with a rating of 2 or 3 for which you would like some resolution. Ask God to help you see <u>what you believe is at stake</u> and any other beliefs you hold in regard to that situation.

2. Be sure to identify what <u>feels</u> true, and ask God what you need to know about the bigger picture. He may direct you to some places in your past where you first developed this fear, so that He can heal the scars from those experiences. Or He may talk to you about how your "truster" got broken, or He may direct you somewhere else. Follow His lead.

3. Begin writing about your fear and why it feels true to you. Then ask God to speak into your heart as you continue to explore your issue in writing.

Session 11 Sailing Practice – Ongoing

1. Focus on the goodness of God each morning and night (Appreciating the Goodness of God).
2. Listen to the Spirit teach you about abiding in John 14-15 (Directly Interacting).

Session 11 Sailing Practice – Healing our Fears

- Pay attention to any feelings of anxiety this week.
- Identify a teachable moment in regard to fear and ask God for His perspective.
- Write out your conversation with God below.

Additional Ways to Deal With Fear

Find someone who is not afraid of what you are afraid of, and talk about your fear.

Find others who have dealt with similar fear and ask them to tell you about their healing process.

Celebrate small steps toward better vision and/or courage.

When you experience fearful circumstances, find your safe person as soon as possible and let them help you return to quiet.

Additional Reading on Recovering from Fear

John Townsend: *Hiding From Love: How to Change the Withdrawal Patterns that Isolate and Imprison You* (Zondervan: Grand Rapids) 1996

Ship's Log – Session 11

For most of my life I believed very deeply in Murphy's law: "*Whatever can go wrong, will go wrong.*" Not that I meant to or wanted to believe this; it just seemed true. Every time I thought I was going to do well, every time I thought something really good would happen, Murphy showed up and proved his theorem was the law of my life.

Interestingly, I never thought of this as fear. It was more of a certainty. When something went badly I would often say to myself, "Well, what did you expect?" The times when it surfaced as fear or anxiety was when I was on the verge of achieving something important to me. I would wonder, "Will this be another one of those things where the rug gets pulled out from under me at the last minute?" Sometimes, I would deliberately <u>not</u> pray for what I wanted, because I was afraid of being disappointed in God as well as my circumstances.

Even after several years of engaging with God for healing, there were remnants of this little pest still hanging around at the time when my first book was printed, and it makes for kind of a funny story.

October 2008 was a very trying month, because I could barely wait for the arrival of my first shipment of books, *The Truth About Lies and Lies About Truth*. When the day finally arrived for the books to be delivered, I set up my laptop near the front window so I could see when the truck came. Believe me, I was ready. All day long I could hear every truck within two blocks, and each one would get me stirred up and wondering if that was the truck I was waiting for.

Eleven o'clock came and went. Twelve. One. I rechecked the tracking number on the website. Yes, they were supposed to deliver today. Two o'clock. I begin to wonder, "What if they don't come today? What if they deliver them to the wrong address? What if they were damaged in shipment? What if ...?"

Finally, it dawned on me that I was really a mess and I needed to talk to God about this. So I pulled out my journal and started to write. Suddenly, the irony of my situation hit me full force, and I burst out laughing. Here I was waiting for this book I had written on how to be healed of the lies we believe that wreak havoc with our lives, and I was sitting here completely convinced that Murphy's law was for real! I have no doubt that God has a tremendous sense of humor – but this was unbelievably funny!

So my next question to God was, "How do I <u>not</u> believe in Murphy? I see how utterly crazy this is, but I'm still afraid they are going to lose my books!" That was when He pointed out my broken "truster." Wow. It was really broken. "I need you God, even more than I thought." As we continued our time together, He comforted me and reassured me that He held me in His heart.

He went on to remind me that He was big enough to restore things even if they went poorly, which helped me understand better how His restorative means of safety could create more trust in me. At that point I was ready to go back to work in front of the window, knowing in my heart God was with me and would stay with me no matter what happened that day. And as it turned out, I had reason to rejoice before the day was out, not only for some important healing moments, but for my books as well!

David Takle
Sailor Apprentice

SESSION 12 – TWO KINDS OF MATURITY
INTEGRATING CHRISTIAN FORMATION AND HUMAN DEVELOPMENT[12]

God designed human beings to grow and develop in certain ways whether or not they are Christians. Unsaved people experience real love, learn how to regulate their emotions, how to make friends, and how to resolve conflict. They can be generous and altruistic, relate well under stress, and show many other characteristics that we often ascribe to *spiritual* maturity. It is not even unusual to find non-Christians who can do some of these things better that a lot of Christians.

If all desirable human development depended on whether or not we were Christians, this would not be so. This suggests that there are clearly some areas of growth for which God has given responsibility to human beings, areas that can be achieved by human means. For example, Christians sometimes view certain skills such as patience as purely spiritual virtues. But the truth is non-Christians can learn patience quite well. So although having the peace of God rest upon you may greatly increase your patience, it is clear that God has given human beings the capacity to learn patience.

This brings to mind certain questions:
- What areas of growth are within the capability of human beings?
- How do those areas differ from what we must receive from God?
- How do we develop maturity in those areas for which we are responsible?
- How are they related to spiritual development?

The way we understand these issues really matters.

This session will describe some of the ways we believe God designed people to grow up and mature. In particular, we will be looking at a model of maturity that was developed some years ago at Shepherd's House which helps to explain how people get stuck in areas where they seem to need more than healing prayer in order to continue growing. Apparently, God does not do for us what He designed us to learn from one another. How this all fits together helps us to understand what kinds of tools we need for differing kinds of problems.

There are several reasons why we need to know the difference between human maturity and spiritual maturity. First, it helps us separate our part from God's part in growing up. Second, when we experience difficulty in certain areas of life, we will be able to apply human resources to human problems and seek God for spiritual problems. Getting these mixed up can cause a lot of frustration and harm. Finally, knowing the difference between these two areas helps us to read the Bible better, because God's Word talks about both kinds of maturity. If we assume the Bible only talks about spiritual issues, we can get very confused about what God expects from us and what God does in us that we cannot do.

We hope you find this session both fascinating and enlightening.

---

12 Material on human maturity is taken from: *The Complete Guide to Living With Men* by E. James Wilder

[Video: Session 12 – Part 1]

Recap of *Forming*
- 11 Sessions on training how to receive from God what we need for life.
- Opportunities to engage with God.
  - In-session exercises.
  - Between-session exercises.
- Life-long pursuit of God.
  - *Forming* was intended as an <u>introduction</u> to point the way toward effective spiritual growth. Taking a course does not grow us up, spiritually. That comes from building a relationship with God and continually engaging with Him.

Two Aspects to Maturity
- Spiritual Maturity.

  Developing the character of Christ
  in the context of a growing relationship with Him.

  - **Received** experientially.
  - Through engaging with **God**.
  - By learning to engage with Him (personally and corporately)
    so <u>He</u> can change our heart and mind.
  - Becoming increasingly **dependent** on God.

- Human Maturity.

  Relating to others with competence and joy
  in the context of increasingly complex relationships.

  - **Achieved** experientially.
  - Through interaction with **people**.
  - By learning developmental tasks as infant, child, adult, parent, elder.
    Receiving what we need from others in order to learn these tasks.
  - Becoming increasingly **interdependent** with one another.

Most of us have been taught that **human** maturity has to do with becoming more and more autonomous. We have also been taught that **spiritual** maturity happens from trying hard to be a good Christian. Both of these views are mistaken.

Human Maturity (restated)
Ability to manage increasingly complex relationships, competently and joyfully.

Notice that this has nothing to do with becoming independent, becoming more autonomous, or "standing on your own two feet".

How We Mature   Notes

This is a highly interactive, interpersonal, developmental process.

- **Needs** must be met by other people in order to accomplish the necessary tasks.
- **Tasks** must be learned experientially.
  - Observing others who are living well. Listening to stories of others.
  - Making our own attempts to master the tasks.
  - Being mentored through trial and error – we learn through practice.

This maturing process is broken down by stages of development. The needs and tasks are different for each developmental stage.

The stages outlined below provide a bird's eye view of human development. Please note that the ages listed represent the earliest that anyone can enter these stages. Many people do not get enough help to accomplish the tasks needed to move on to the next stage of maturity. So it is possible to remain at infant or child level even though we are much older. We can also miss a few tasks along the way that we did not get help with, which leaves us with "holes" in our maturity.

Infant (ages 0-3)

Infant's main job is to learn how to receive with joy.

- Infant's needs are care-giver's responsibility, and needs are met without asking.
- Family members accommodate the infant's needs (not the other way around).

Compare to infants in families where parents resent demands of parenting.

- Some learn that Mom and Dad have nothing to give.
- Some learn that their needs are an imposition on others.
- Some are born with a job, such as to make Mom and Dad happy.

We cannot learn how to receive unless someone is joyfully giving to us.

Child (ages 4-12)

Learns how to identify needs and get some of their own needs met. This is about emotional and relational self-care more than physical skills.

- How to ask for help. How to advocate for themselves.
- How to get others to understand them.
- Develop personal resources and talents.

Need mentoring and help with attempts and guesses in order to learn these.

Adult (from 13 to birth of first child)

While a <u>child</u> learns how to care for their own needs (or take turns), <u>adults</u> must learn how to meet the needs of two people at the same time.

- Develop <u>mutuality</u> in relationships.
- Develop a group identity, which means moving beyond the idea of "you" and "I" toward a sense that "we" form a single unit.

Lack of adult level maturity is a major reason relationships fail.

Parent (from birth of first child to when the last child leaves home)

Learns how to meet the needs of infants and children unilaterally with joy.

- Helps children learn to meet their own needs.
- Non-mutual relationship (very one-sided in meeting needs).
- Giving with joy – not resentful or merely out of obligation.

Becoming a parent without reaching parent maturity can be serious.

- Resentment about what children require.
- Expect children to meet some of their needs.
- Unable to train children in areas the parents were never trained in.

Elder (after last child leaves home)

Relatively rare, even though many people try to fill this role.

- Learns how to foster community relationships with joy.
- Able to mentor all stages of development.
- Helps community develop group identity.

Having an elder <u>role</u> without the earned maturity can be disastrous for the group.

How We Mature as Human Beings

This is an interpersonal, highly interactive developmental process.

- **Needs** must be met by other people in order for us to learn the necessary tasks.
- **Tasks** must be learned experientially.

See chart on page 150 for a summary of needs and tasks by maturity level.

[Video: Session 12 – Part 2]

Human Maturity and Spiritual Maturity

- <u>Human maturity</u> is primarily *earned* through interaction with community,
    aided by our connection with God.
- <u>Spiritual maturity</u> is primarily *received* through interaction with God,
    aided by our connections with others (see corporate practices in Sessions 6,7,8).

Each impacts the other, incrementally.

The Bible speaks about both kinds of maturity.

  (That's one reason we get confused about trying to *earn* spiritual maturity.)

Interdependent Growth

- As human growth is *achieved*, it opens ways to *receive* more spiritual life.
- As spiritual growth is *received* from interacting with God,
    human development becomes more *achievable*.

Examples of how <u>human</u> maturity can aid our <u>spiritual</u> development.

(1) Growing my capacity for discomfort (a human task) opens new space for talking
    to God about my wounded areas.

(2) Knowing how to quiet my mind (a human task) greatly aids my ability to enter into conversations with God and to hear Him better.

(3) Knowing how to do things that I don't feel like doing at the moment (a human task) helps me persist in seeking God.

Examples of how <u>spiritual</u> maturity can aid our <u>human</u> development.

(1) Learning how God can meet my inner needs aids the human task of learning how to tame my cravings.

(2) Discovering more of how God sees me can greatly assist the human task of returning to joy from shame.

(3) A strong sense of God's presence gives me a lot of security, which then helps me learn various human tasks such as staying relational during a rupture.

Missing Maturity

- Lack of *spiritual* maturity can lead to ...
  - Self-reliance on our own abilities to do God's job in our life.
  - Lack of healing we might need in order to continue our development.
  - Limited discernment in life.
- Lack of *human* maturity can lead to ...
  - Relational situations that are too complex for us.
  - Attempting to apply spiritual solutions to areas of human responsibility.
  - Over-spiritualizing or moralizing of developmental and relational issues.

To put it another way:

- If we rely too much on our human ability, we will become frustrated with our lack of spiritual development.
- If we expect God to handle all the complexities of our adult relationships (without doing the work of growing up), we will cause harm to ourselves and others.

Recovery and Human Maturity

- Holes in our maturity are <u>not</u> due to "defective DNA" or moral failure on our part, but from unmet needs and inadequate training.
  - Not an issue for shame or self-deprecation.
- You can only learn from those who know.
  - Learning by example.
  - Learning through stories of the experiences of others.
  - Getting help with our attempts.
- We need to find people who are "upstream" from us
     and learn from them about these issues.

A Vision of What Church Can Be

"Speaking the truth in love, we will in <u>all things grow up</u> into him ... From him the whole body ... <u>grows and builds itself up in love, as each part does its work</u>" (Eph.4:15-16).

Notes

Stages of Human Development / Maturity

Stage	Needs to be Met by Others	Tasks to be Accomplished
Infant	Strong, loving bonds with parents Important needs met without asking Adults synchronize* to the infant's emotions and needs Help regulating their distress and emotions To be seen "with the eyes of heaven"	Learn how to receive with joy – develop trust Organize self into person through imitation Learn how to regulate and quiet every emotion Learn how to return to joy from every emotion Learn how to remain the same person in different contexts Learn how to rest
Child	Help sorting out feelings, imagination, and reality Feedback on guesses, attempts, failures Help doing what he/she does not want to Love that is not earned To be taught the big picture of life	Develop personal resources and talents Learn to ask for help and for what they need Take care of self (relationally and emotionally) Learn self-expression Develop persistence for doing hard things Tame cravings – learn what satisfies See self through eyes of heaven
Adult	Opportunity to form bonds with peers Inclusion by the adult community Observe adults using power fairly Opportunity for important involvement in community Guidance for personal impact on community life Opportunities for mutual relationships	Learn to take care of two or more people at once Discover main characteristics of his/her heart Proclaim and defend personal and group identity Remain stable in distress Bring self and others back to joy together Develop personal style reflecting heart Learn to protect others from self (life-giving use of power)

* When adults synchronize to an infant, it means they accommodate the needs of the infant and attune to the infant's emotional state. This is in contrast to narcissistic parents or parenting styles that attempt to force the infant to match the parent's emotions and schedules.

Stage	Needs to be Met by Others	Tasks to be Accomplished
Parent	Encouragement and guidance from elders Peer review with other parents Secure and orderly community	Learn to give without needing to receive in return (non-mutual) Learn to meet children's needs with joy Joyfully, help children with their tasks Protect the family unit Serve and enjoy family
Elder	A community in which to belong Recognition by the community A proper place in community structure Opportunities to be involved in lives of community members	Hospitality How to joyfully give life to those outside of family Nurture community identity and purpose Able to guide group through difficulty and return group back to joy

An underlying assumption of this model is that **joy** and **shalom** are our natural state!
Joy is more than being happy. It is a relational emotion that means: (a) someone is glad to be with me; and/or (b) I am glad to see life-giving things happen for people, and they are glad for me.
Shalom means everything is as it should be, in the right amount and the right intensity.
We were designed to live in joy and shalom!

There are also a few developmental tasks that cross all stages. The main one is developing an increasing **capacity** for emotional intensity, whether joy or some negative emotion such as fear, anger, sadness, shame, or hopelessness. Our capacity grows best by building joy and peace with other people, which is our natural state as God designed us. Capacity allows us to remain stable and relational across a broad spectrum of life experience, rather than become disoriented and non-relational under stress.

Data and concepts for table taken from: E James Wilder: *Complete Guide to Living With Men, 2004*
Note: this is only a partial list and does not include all of the characteristics of maturity for each stage.
(We realize many of these phrases may not be self-explanatory. Please see the book for more information)

Exercise 12 – Talking With God About Our Human Maturity

Take a few minutes to review the infant and child level maturity needs and tasks. Then talk to God about the following areas. Also, feel free to talk to Him about any thoughts you have along these lines as well.

- What are some significant blank spots in my maturity?
- How do you see my maturity, God?
- Who are You leading me to for help with my maturity?
- In what ways have these missing pieces resulted in other issues for which I need to find healing?

Session 12 Sailing Practice – Ongoing

1. Focus on the goodness of God each morning and night (Appreciating the Goodness of God).
2. Listen to the Spirit teach you about abiding in John 14-15 (Directly Interacting).

Session 12 Sailing Practice – Exercise for Long-Term Growth

1. Identify a maturity task that you are not yet doing well.
2. Identify at least two others who do this well.
3. Ask them to tell you about experiences where they have needed this skill and what it is like for them to walk through these experiences, including what is going on for them mentally and emotionally.

Additional Reading on Integrating Human Maturity and Spiritual Maturity

E. James Wilder: *The Complete Guide to Living With Men* (Shepherd's House: Pasadena) 2006

Peter Scazzero: *Emotionally Healthy Spirituality: Unleash a Revolution in Your Life In Christ* (Thomas Nelson: Nashville) 2011

Friesen, Jim Wilder, Ann Bierling, Rick Koepcke, Maribeth Poole: *The Life Model: Living From the Heart Jesus Gave You* (Shepherd's House: Pasadena) 2001

Ship's Log – Session 12

Every once in a while I am privileged to witness someone who can navigate complex situations so well that I am truly amazed at how they do what they do. When I see them manage a difficult experience with such little effort, I think, "How did you know what to do?" And I never forget what I learn in those moments.

Sadly, I also witness moments every bit as shocking at the other end of the spectrum. It might be a parent, decimating their child with words that cut and mutilate their fragile soul. Or a co-worker who deliberately lies to their boss about what is going on in the shop in order to get ahead. Or even a senior pastor who fires an associate pastor because he feels threatened by the way church members are warming up to the younger man's leadership style. These are tragic, painful events to see up close. And in some cases the damage that is done goes on for years in the lives of those impacted by these things.

I know in some circles such tragedies are judged as moral failures. But the truth is that in many such events, people have simply never earned the level of maturity necessary to handle the complexities they are dealing with. For example, the parent I mentioned is incredibly needy. Without meaning to, she expects her children to give her what she never got from her own parents. She stopped growing a long time ago, and has no idea how to fill the holes in her soul. So whenever her children "let her down" she reacts with all the rage of a three-year-old who is feeling abandoned.

Now compare that to a situation I remember in which a mature response made all the difference. A friend of mine went to the post office to mail a package. When she got up to the window, things did not initially go well. Apparently the worker was in a foul mood, and she took one look at the package and pushed it back into the hands of my friend, saying something like, "You can't mail that! It's wrapped all wrong!"

As my friend was telling me this story, I immediately had visions in my head of either quietly slinking out the door or else giving the postal worker a piece of my mind. But my friend's story did not go that way at all. She looked at the woman behind the counter and said, "Oh, I'm so glad you know how to wrap these things. Can you show me what I need to do so this can go through the mail?" It caught the postal worker completely off guard. She changed her attitude, explained how to wrap the package and gave her a few extra tips as well. My friend thanked her and went home to re-wrap her parcel.

I was astounded and asked, "How did you do that? Why didn't you do what I would have done?" And as my friend described this event for me again, I began to understand that this is what it looks like when you know who you are, and you keep the boundaries in place, and you stay relational even when someone else does not. It had never dawned on me that you could maintain your dignity without having to defend yourself in a spot like that. I learned a lot from her story.

I guess maturity really does matter. When we get help to learn the skills we need to have in order to mature, life simply works better. And if I pay attention to others who know how to do some of these things, I can learn these tasks even if I'm already a "grown up."

David Takle
Sailor Apprentice

APPENDIX

This section contains:

1. An extra copy of each Session Exercise used in the book (not including Sailing Practice)

2. Bibliography

3. An Index of Articles on various topics

Exercise 1 – Isaiah 55 and Sailing

This passage is a beautiful, poetic message of *receiving from God what we need for life*. Since we are looking for how God can bring life to us in ways we cannot achieve on our own, this passage is very relevant.

Enter into this passage with all your heart, yearning for more of the spiritual food God has for you. Listen for God's leading as you reflect and write. Since there are no 'right' or 'wrong' answers, be as honest as you can about your thoughts and feelings as you pay attention to how these verses impact your heart and mind. Ask God for what you need to see and hear. Do not worry about writing well or only writing what you think is important. Simply begin writing as you are reading and reflecting – whatever comes to mind.

1. Read the verses below from Isaiah 55.
2. Reflect on what is God saying to you about <u>*you*</u>, about "<u>*receiving*</u>," and about <u>*God's Heart for you.*</u>
3. Write down the words and phrases that most capture your attention, whatever emotional reactions you have, and any longings these verses stir up in you. Do not wait until you have a well-formed response. Simply write whatever comes to mind. (This is not a test to see how well you can formulate an idea. We are practicing <u>active spiritual reflection</u>).

Isaiah 55 (selected portions)   (NRSV)

Hey, everyone who thirsts, come to the waters;
and you that have no money, come, buy and eat!
Come, buy wine and milk without money and without price.
[2] Why do you spend your money for that which is not bread,
and your labor for that which does not satisfy?
Listen carefully to me, and eat what is good, and delight yourselves in rich food.
[3] Incline your ear, and come to me; listen, so that you may live.
[10] For as the rain and the snow come down from heaven, and do not return there until they have watered the earth, making it bring forth and sprout, giving seed to the sower and bread to the eater,
[11] so shall my word be that goes out from my mouth;
it shall not return to me empty, but it shall accomplish that which I purpose,
and succeed in the thing for which I sent it.
[12] For you shall go out in joy, and be led back in peace;
the mountains and the hills before you shall burst into song,
and all the trees of the field shall clap their hands.

Exercise 2A – Practicing Appreciation

--- Part 1 --- Identifying Appreciation Moments   (10 minutes)
This exercise will highlight the value of practicing appreciation, in and of itself.
(1) Identify 3 things in your life for which you are truly grateful. Choose things you can feel genuine appreciation for (not things for which you think you *should* feel appreciation). These do not have to be explicitly "spiritual" in nature. Here are some ideas to help stir your memories:
   • A person who has meant a great deal to you (friend, mentor, family member).
   • An experience you have had (or event you have attended) that was very rich and memorable.
   • A place you have lived (or visited) that has special meaning for you.
(2) Write out each "appreciation moment" in 3-4 sentences, stating enough to help you identify it, express the feelings you have about it, and tell why it means so much to you.
(3) Give each item on the list a name – one word or short phrase.

Example:
I still remember my first trip to the Grand Canyon and how overwhelmed I was by its beauty and grandeur. As I walked up to the edge, I was struck speechless by the immensity of it all. When I picture myself standing at the edge of the canyon, my whole body reacts and my heart goes to total wonder. I call this my *Grand Canyon Moment*.

--- Part 2 --- Sharing Appreciation with Others   (6 minutes)
Pair up with one other person. Allow three minutes for each of you to share one of your appreciation moments with the other person. Be sure to go beyond your short description and include ...
   • how it impacts your mind and body to recall your appreciation moment.
   • what you were feeling a few minutes ago, prior to Part 1 of the exercise.
   • what you experienced as you wrote out your appreciation moment.
After each story, the listener can reflect back a sentence or two about how they were impacted by the other person's story.

Exercise 2B – Appreciation Moments With God

> "Let the peace of Christ rule in your hearts, to which indeed you were called in one body; **and be thankful**. Let the word of Christ richly dwell within you, with all wisdom teaching and admonishing one another with psalms and hymns and spiritual songs, singing **with thankfulness in your hearts to God**" (Col.3:15-16 NASB).

Exercise 2A was about practicing appreciation in regard to any aspect of our life.
This exercise will focus on appreciation moments with God.

1. Recall one of your appreciation moments, and allow yourself to feel appreciation for a full minute.

2. Now take a moment to remember some way you have experienced God or His goodness toward you. Try to choose something that had a significant impact on you and with which you can still reconnect emotionally. (This is not merely a cognitive exercise). This should be something quite experiential or relational in nature, and *not* a material blessing you received, such as when you got a new car or job or money (unless it was essential in some way, such as after a significant loss).
Some examples:
   • Being aware of the greatness of God in creation (mountains, ocean, or even a local park).
   • Feeling close to God through music (example: "How Great is Our God...").
   • While reading Psalm 23 or Isaiah 55 or your favorite passage.
   • The wonder of God you feel while watching your child sleeping.
   • Experiencing a glimpse of God's goodness in someone you know or have met.
   • When you were comforted and encouraged by God at a difficult time in your life.
   • An inspired message you heard.
   • A God-breathed word spoken to you by a friend at the right time.
   • Excitement and energy you felt in an important spiritual experience.

3. When you have selected a memory:
   • Focus your mind on that experience.
   • Try to engage that memory with your heart as well as your mind. (What was it like to be there?)
   • Allow yourself to feel your appreciation for God's goodness in that experience.
   • Hold the appreciation in your heart and savor this moment with God.

4. After a few minutes, ask God if there is anything else He wants you to know about this moment. Wait a couple of minutes to see if anything else comes to mind as you reflect on your appreciation moment with God.

5. Take at least five minutes to write out your own psalm of praise and appreciation (use next page).

Exercise 3A – Quiet and Focus

Psalm 27 contains some very rich imagery that comes out of the writer's deep desire to be with God. He is probably out in the desert somewhere, imagining what it would be like to live in the Temple 24 hours a day, 7 days a week.

1. Allow yourself to relax. Recall an appreciation moment.
2. Invite God to reveal Himself to you and to open your heart to His presence.
3. Read the excerpt from Psalm 27 below.
   Try to join the Psalmist as he longs to be in the presence of God.
4. Record any pictures, impressions, emotions or words that come to mind.

> "One thing I asked of the Lord, that will I seek after; to live in the house of the Lord all the days of my life; **to behold the beauty of the Lord**, and to inquire in his temple.... 'Come' my heart says, 'seek His face!' Your face, Lord, do I seek" (Ps.27:4,8).

Exercise 3B – Listening to God and the Word

Psalm 139 is a beautiful expression of the psalmist's trust that _God knows him and loves him completely at the same time,_ and no matter where he goes or how far he strays he can never get lost.

(Please note: this Psalm has often been misunderstood as a fearful vision of God scrutinizing the psalmist, but it is actually a joyful expression of his total trust in God's goodness.)

1. Take a minute or two to quiet and focus. Recall an appreciation moment with God.
2. Ask God to show you His heart regarding the text below, and listen as you read.
3. Let some phrase or word capture your attention, allow it to fill your imagination, and ask God to reveal whatever He wants you to see in regard to that phrase.
4. Write down whatever feelings and impressions come to mind. (Use the space below and the next page.)

Do not try to cover the whole passage or worry too much about whether the words you write are your words or God's at this point. Simply begin your reflection with the anticipation that God is with you and will join you in this process.

Psalm 139

[1] O Lord, you have searched me and known me. [2] You know when I sit down and when I rise up; You discern my thoughts from far away. [3] You search out my path and my lying down, and are acquainted with all my ways. [4] Even before a word is on my tongue, O Lord, you know it completely. [5] You hem me in, behind and before, and lay your hand upon me.

[6] Such knowledge is too wonderful for me; it is so high that I cannot attain it.

[12] Even the darkness is not dark to you; the night is as bright as the day, for darkness is as light to you.

[13] For it was you who formed my inward parts; you knit me together in my mother's womb. [14] I praise you, for I am fearfully and wonderfully made; Wonderful are your works; that I know very well.

[23] Search me, O God, and know my heart; test me and know my thoughts. [24] See if there is any hurtful way in me, and lead me in the way everlasting.

Exercise 4A – Remember Psalm 139

One of the best ways to connect with God is to recall a previous conversation we had with Him or a previous time of reflection.

"I will call to mind the deeds of the Lord ... I will meditate on all your works" (Ps.77:11-12 NRSV).

1. Spend a few minutes quieting and remembering your previous reflection on Psalm 139 (Exercise 3B). If God gave you some life-giving perspective during that exercise, re-read your notes and recall what He revealed to you.
2. Read the excerpt from Psalm 139 below, taken from the New Living Translation. Reading from a different translation often helps to foster new ways of seeing the passage.
3. Consider what it means to be totally known and loved at the same time.
4. Write out your heart's response.

"O Lord, you have examined my heart and know everything about me...You chart the path ahead of me and tell me where to stop and rest...You both precede and follow me. You place your hand of blessing on my head. Such knowledge is too wonderful for me, too great for me to know!" (NLT).

Exercise 4B – Discussing an Important Issue With God

In the previous session, we spent some time in conversation with the Spirit of God, asking Him to open our eyes to whatever He wanted to show us regarding Psalm 139. Using Scripture is a great way for us to begin a conversation with God. But we can also use a life issue as the starting point for our conversation.

1. Take a few moments to quiet and focus. Rest as much as possible in the presence of God. Recall an appreciation moment.

2. Ask God one of the following questions:
   (a) God, how do You see our relationship?
   If this question raises a lot of anxiety or defensiveness in you, or if nothing at all comes to mind, then consider this question instead:
   (b) God, what do I need to know about You that would make the first question more addressable?
   or possibly:
   (c) God, what can you tell me about the fear and defensiveness I feel when I think about asking you how You see our relationship?

3. Write out whatever feelings come up and whatever you sense God may be saying to you. (Don't try to guess what He would say, let it come to you.) Write as you feel led, and when the stream slows down, ask God to draw you to whatever it is He wants you to really focus on.
   If nothing comes to mind, begin by telling God how the relationship looks from your point of view. After sharing your perspective for a few minutes, ask Him if He sees it any differently.
   If your conversation slows down but does not feel resolved, go back to exercise 3B and ask God how Psalm 139 can help you see more of how He cares about you.

Exercise 5A – Quiet

It is easy to get caught up in the demands of the world around us and forget that we live in the presence of God. Allowing yourself to rest with God is a valuable way to remember <u>who you are</u>, <u>whose you are</u> and what is truly important.

Ask the Spirit of God to calm your body and soul and to open your heart to His presence.
Read the verses below and allow yourself to feel the peace of God.

> "He makes me lie down in green pastures; He leads me beside **quiet** waters" (Ps.23:2).

> "My soul, wait in **silence** for God only, For my hope is from Him" (Ps.62:5).

For the next few minutes simply rest in Him.

Exercise 5B – Incorporating More Grace Into My Life

For this exercise we are going to spend some time talking to God about an area in our life where we need to experience more of God's work and less of our own direct effort.

1. Ask God if there is one area below He would like to talk to you about.
2. Spend some time reflecting and listening to what God wants to reveal to you about this matter.
3. Use the space below to write out your reflection and any thoughts revealed by God.

- Is there an area in my life that I have been expecting to correct on my own?
- Are there ways I have been expecting my knowledge of doctrine or my involvement in the church to make me a better Christian? How would living by grace impact any of this process?
- Is there another person I have judged too harshly? God, how do You see this person?
- God, is there something I have felt too ashamed of to talk to You about? What do I need to know about You that will change how I think You see me?

Exercise 6A – Practicing Appreciation in Joy

"Be filled with the Spirit, speaking to one another in psalms and hymns and spiritual songs, singing and making melody with your heart to the Lord; always giving thanks for all things in the name of our Lord Jesus Christ" (Eph.5:18-20, NASB).

This will be a fairly short exercise of quieting and focusing. Our goal here is to become more aware of God's presence with us and to appreciate His goodness toward us. As we begin to feel gratitude and joy, we want to simply enjoy our closeness with God.

- Accept in faith that God's presence is completely enveloping you at this moment, permeating every cell of your body.
- Turn your heart toward Him as you quiet your mind.
- Envision God enjoying this moment with you.
- Allow yourself to rejoice in His presence and goodness.

Enjoy the moment!

(If several minutes pass without any sense of appreciation, reflect back on a prior time when you aware of the presence of God, and allow yourself to feel appreciation for that experience).

Exercise 6B – Writing a Psalm of Appreciation in Distress

While there are times when we feel appreciation quite naturally, we also have times and areas of life where we do not feel at all appreciative. We find this to be true in the Psalms, as well. This exercise will begin with an area in which we feel burdened, and move toward a place of trust and comfort for which we can feel appreciation. We are not asking God to resolve any issues at this time, but to help us arrive at a place where we can appreciate His presence and goodness in the midst of our difficulty. In the process, we will write out a short Psalm that has elements of both our distress and appreciation.

1. Spend 2 minutes quieting and focusing on the presence of God.
   • If possible, find some place of appreciation (unrelated to your area of distress) that you can acknowledge and feel.

2. Spend 5 minutes writing to God about an area of distress in your life.
   • Consider asking God what area to address.
   • Work / Home / Relative / Friend / Health / Finances.
   • Include the situation, emotions, affected relationships, and whatever seems to be at stake.

3. Spend 4 minutes allowing God to restore comfort to you in whatever way He desires.
   • Actively seek His presence with you and His love for you.
   • Welcome any new perspectives He might want to show you.
   • Continue to record what comes to mind during this time.

4. Spend 2 minutes writing out your appreciation for God's response to you and His comfort.

Exercise 6C – Telling Our Appreciation Stories

In this exercise you will share your experience in regard to Seeking Appreciation in Distress in Exercise 6B. If you did not reach a place of appreciation during this exercise, feel free to share another experience you have had in which you were able to be comforted by God.

1. Gather in groups of 3 (or in pairs).
2. Everyone <u>tells an appreciation story</u> about how God met them in Exercise 6B.
   • About 3 minutes per person.
   • Focus on the joy part of the story. Include only a very brief reference to the type of distress.
   • Help your listeners know what it was like to experience God's comfort.
   • Include how your thoughts, emotions, and body changed as God met you.

Exercise 7 – Reading With Expectation

Enjoy a few minutes <u>Listening to the Word</u>, while fully appreciating His presence with you and anticipating His interaction with you.

- Find a place of appreciation and hold that for a full minute.
- Prayerfully anticipate that God intends for this passage to be food for your soul.
- Read through the passage below slowly (at least twice) with the expectation that you will experience:
  - Paul's hope for you as a Christian.
  - Fresh insights about God, life, or yourself.
  - Internal resistance or confrontation.
  - Deeper yearning for a stronger relationship.
- Some things you might pay attention to and discuss with God:
  - Any word or phrase that catches your attention.
  - Reactions in your body (emotional, physical).
  - Any longings that are stirred up in you.
  - Any leading or change of direction you feel drawn to.

Begin writing as you reflect and listen.

"That He would grant you, according to the riches of his glory, to be strengthened with might through his Spirit in the inner man, that Christ may dwell in your hearts through faith; that you, being rooted and grounded in love, may be able to comprehend with all the saints what is the width and length and depth and height – to know the love of Christ which passes knowledge; that you may be filled with all the fullness of God. Now to Him who is able to do exceedingly abundantly above all that we ask or think, according to the power that works in us" (Eph.3:16-20, NKJV).

Exercise 8 – What If You Were There?[13]

1. Read the passage below.
2. Try to enter the drama as much as possible as a participant in the event. Walk through the story as if you are actually there as (1) the woman, (2) the Pharisee, (3) Jesus, or (4) one of the dinner guests. How is your experience shaped by your character's particular perspective? What would you see, hear, smell, taste, feel, touch? What would you notice? What would be memorable about this event that you would remember a week or a month later? Six months later?
3. If you are in a large group, divide up into four smaller groups and assign one of these characters to each group. After about 20 minutes, have each group report back to the larger group what they discovered about their character's experience. Try to take into consideration anything you know about the customs and expectations of Jewish culture at that time.

Luke 7: 36-50   (New King James translation)

Then one of the Pharisees asked Him to eat with him. And He went to the Pharisee's house, and sat down to eat. And behold, a woman in the city who was a sinner, when she knew that Jesus sat at the table in the Pharisee's house, brought an alabaster flask of fragrant oil, and stood at his feet behind Him weeping; and she began to wash his feet with her tears, and wiped them with the hair of her head; and she kissed his feet and anointed them with the fragrant oil. Now when the Pharisee who had invited Him saw this, he spoke to himself saying, "This Man, if He were a prophet, would know who and what manner of woman this is who is touching Him, for she is a sinner."

And Jesus answered and said to him, "Simon, I have something to say to you."

So he said, "Teacher, say it."

"There was a certain creditor who had two debtors. One owed five hundred denarii and the other fifty. And when they had nothing with which to repay, he freely forgave them both. Tell Me, therefore, which of them will love him more?"

Simon answered and said, "I suppose the one whom he forgave more."

And He said to him, "You have rightly judged." Then He turned to the woman and said to Simon, "Do you see this woman? I entered your house; you gave Me no water for My feet, but she has washed My feet with her tears and wiped them with the hair of her head. You gave Me no kiss, but this woman has not ceased to kiss My feet since the time I came in. You did not anoint My head with oil, but this woman has anointed My feet with fragrant oil. Therefore I say to you, her sins, which are many, are forgiven, for she loved much. But to whom little is forgiven, the same loves little."

Then He said to her, "Your sins are forgiven."

And those who sat at the table with Him began to say to themselves, "Who is this who even forgives sins?"

Then He said to the woman, "Your faith has saved you. Go in peace."

---

13 The idea for this exercise comes from Joel Warne in *The Intimate Journey*

Exercise 9A – Perceptions and Observations About Life

For each of the items below ask, **How <u>often</u> do I feel or think this way?**
Rate each one from 0 to 5 using the scale below. If a particular item seems dependent upon particular people or circumstances, feel free to make a note next to the item and give it a second rating as well.

0=never   1=rarely   2=occasionally   3=sometimes   4=often   5=most of the time

___ I am afraid of what God wants from me   ___ I worry about finances

___ I think God is disappointed in me   ___ I'm really hard on myself

___God seems very distant from me   ___ Evil seems more powerful than good

___ I feel angry at God about things that have happened to me

___ I have doubts about God's interest or concern for me

___ I'm better off alone than trying to get close to others

___ I have places in my life where I feel stuck and cannot seem to change

___ I feel judgmental or contemptuous toward others

___ I compare myself to others and feel as if I don't measure up

___ I seem to need everyone to like me and/or approve of me

___ There are people that I'm not sure I can ever forgive

___ I have trouble "forgiving myself" for mistakes I have made

___ I am afraid of making mistakes or failing at things I try

___ I am surprised by how negative my reaction can be to certain situations

___ I have painful regrets about choices I have made

___ I believe negative feedback more than positive

There is no scoring for this survey. The purpose is to call attention to areas which may indicate the presence of underlying beliefs that God wants to change.

Exercise 9B – Healing Mistaken Beliefs

The goal of this exercise is to engage with God very directly and ask Him to shine His light of truth on an internalized belief that you hold.

1. Choose one item from Exercise 9A with a rating of 2 or 3 that you want to talk to God about. Make sure that it is an issue you can connect with emotionally.
2. Begin by recalling an appreciation moment. Ask God to open your heart to His presence and voice.
3. Ask God to help you remember a situation when the item you selected felt particularly true.
4. When you have a a sense of both God's involvement and the item you are considering, ask God <u>what He wants to reveal to you</u> about that experience:
   • If there are internalized beliefs you already hold in your heart that need healing.
   • Any perspectives of life or experience of God you are missing and need from Him.

Record your thoughts and impressions as you ponder this issue. Remember, sensing God's truth is not passive. Stay engaged, while exploring the subject and listening at the same time.

Exercise 10A – A Survey of Self-Hate / Self-Rejection Symptoms

For each of the items below ask, **How <u>often</u> do I feel or think this way, or act like this?**

   0=never   1=rarely   2=occasionally   3=sometimes   4=often   5=most of the time

___ I'm really hard on myself about mistakes or oversights

___ I don't like who I am, who I have become

___ I have thoughts of self-destructive actions

___ I despair over my feelings of powerlessness

___ I felt unloved / unwanted by my parents in ways that have not been healed

___ I can allow others grace in ways that I will not allow for myself

___ I think I have an inner saboteur who tries to ruin my life

___ I feel shame or fear when receiving (gifts, help, compliments, comfort)

___ I believe negative feedback more than positive

___ I think that if you knew me better, you wouldn't like me

___ I have been cheated out of having the spouse or income or [whatever] I needed to have

___ I compare myself to others and feel inferior in some important aspects

___ I have very little self-worth   ___ I feel like I can't do anything right

___ I reject compliments   ___ I assume that people will reject me

___ I think God disapproves of me   ___ I am a perfectionist

___ I hide behind a rather strong facade   ___ I wish I had never been born

There is no scoring for this survey. The purpose is to call attention to areas which may indicate the presence of underlying beliefs that God wants to change.

Exercise 10B – Healing From Distorted Self Images

Choose an item from Exercise 10A that has a rating of 2 or 3 that you want to talk to God about.

1. Recall an appreciation moment. Ask God to open your heart to His presence and voice.

2. Ask God to help you remember where you first learned to believe this about yourself.

3. When you have a sense of both God's presence and the thing you are considering,
   ask God what He wants to reveal to you about that belief or perception.
   - What you already hold in your heart that needs healing.
   - Whatever it is that you are missing and need from Him.

Record your thoughts and impressions throughout this time.

Exercise 11A – Naming Our FearsExercise 11A – Naming Our Fears

The items below are things people commonly find fearful, and ways we might describe those fears. Using a scale of 0 to 5, rates the items below according to how strongly you feel fear in regard to each person or thing. Feel free to qualify any of the items, if necessary.

0 = not at all   1 = very minor   2 = somewhat   3 = moderate   4 = strong   5 = extreme

---

Ways We Describe Our Fears

Walking on eggshells	Intimidation	Unease
Unsafe	Foreboding	Anxiety
Distrust	Terror	Dread
Apprehension	Panic	Scary

People, Things, Circumstances

___My boss	___Exposure	___My own anger
___My spouse	___Failure	___Another person's anger
___My parents	___Success	___Shame
___A brother or sister	___Intimacy	___Poor health / Getting sick
___Some other relative	___God's view of me	___Death
___Rejection by others	___God's will for me	___Finances
___Work responsibilities	___Loss of control	___Wasting my life
___Family responsibilities	___Needs not being met	___Making mistakes
___Abandonment	___Physical pain	___My own inner impulses

There is no scoring for this survey. The purpose is to call attention to areas which may indicate the presence of underlying beliefs that God wants to change.

Exercise 11B – Asking God About Our Fear

1. Choose an item on the survey sheet with a rating of 2 or 3 for which you would like some resolution. Ask God to help you see <u>what you believe is at stake</u> and any other beliefs you hold in regard to that situation.

2. Be sure to identify what <u>feels</u> true, and ask God what you need to know about the bigger picture. He may direct you to some places in your past where you first developed this fear, so that He can heal the scars from those experiences. Or He may talk to you about how your "truster" got broken, or He may direct you somewhere else. Follow His lead.

3. Begin writing about your fear and why it feels true to you. Then ask God to speak into your heart as you continue to explore your issue in writing.

Exercise 12 – Talking With God About Our Human Maturity

Take a few minutes to review the infant and child level maturity needs and tasks. Then talk to God about the following areas. Also, feel free to talk to Him about any thoughts you have along these lines as well.

- What are some significant blank spots in my maturity?
- How do you see my maturity, God?
- Who are You leading me to for help with my maturity?
- In what ways have these missing pieces resulted in other issues for which I need to find healing?

Recommended Reading

David Benner: *The Gift of Being Yourself: The Sacred Call to Self-Discovery* (IVP Books: Downers Grove, IL) 2008

David Benner: *Surrender to Love: Discovering the Heart of Christian Spirituality* (IVP Books: Downers Grove, IL) 2003

Friesen, Jim Wilder, Ann Bierling, Rick Koepcke, Maribeth Poole: *The Life Model: Living From the Heart Jesus Gave You* (Shepherd's House: Pasadena) 2001

Wayne Jacobson: *He Loves Me! Learning to Live in the Father's Affection* (Windblown Media: Newbury Park, CA) 2007

Jan Johnson: *When the Soul Listens* (NavPress: Colorado Springs) 1999

Karl Lehman: *Outsmarting Yourself: Catching Your Past Invading the Present and What To Do About It* (This Joy! Books: Libertyville, IL) 2011

Steve McVey: *Grace Walk: What You've Always Wanted in the Christian Life* (Harvest House: Eugene, OR) 2005

J.B. Phillips: *Your God is Too Small* (Touchstone: New York) 1997

James Bryan Smith: *The Good and Beautiful God: Falling in Love with the God Jesus Knows* (IVP Books: Downers Grove, IL) 2009

Theodore Rubin: *Compassion and Self-Hate: An Alternative to Despair* (Touchstone: New York) 1998. (His description and analysis of self-hate are superb, though being a non-Christian author, his solutions are more self-help.)

Peter Scazzero: *Emotionally Healthy Spirituality: Unleash a Revolution in Your Life In Christ* (Thomas Nelson: Nashville) 2011

Gary Smalley: *Change Your Heart, Change Your Life: How Changing What You Believe Will Give You the Great Life You've Always Wanted* (Thomas Nelson: Nashville) 2008

David Takle: *Whispers of My Abba* (Shepherd's House: Pasadena) 2011

David Takle: *The Truth About Lies And Lies About Truth* (Shepherd's House: Pasadena) 2008

David Takle: *Forming: a Work of Grace* (2012)

John Townsend: *Hiding From Love: How to Change the Withdrawal Patterns that Isolate and Imprison You* (Zondervan: Grand Rapids) 1996

E. James Wilder: *The Complete Guide to Living With Men* (Shepherd's House: Pasadena) 2006

Jim Wilder, Chris Coursey: *Share Immanuel* (Shepherd's House: Pasadena) 2010

Dallas Willard: *The Divine Conspiracy: Rediscovering Our Hidden Life in God* (HarperOne: New York) 1998

Dallas Willard: *Hearing God: Developing a Conversational Relationship with God* (IVP Books: Downers Grove, IL) 1999

Dallas Willard: *Renovation of the Heart: Putting on the Character of Christ* (NavPress: Colorado Springs) 2002

Dallas Willard: *The Spirit of the Disciplines: Understanding How God Changes Lives* (HarperOne: New York) 1990

Also please see information available on www.lifemodel.org, especially the help for conversational prayer located at Listen.LifeModel.org.

Other Sources Cited in this Book

Larry Crabb: *The Papa Prayer* (Thomas Nelson: Nashville) 2007

Larry Crabb: *Connecting* (Thomas Nelson: Nashville) 2004

C.S. Lewis: *Screwtape Letters* (Barbour: Uhrichsville, OH) 1990

Chris Thurman: *The Lies We Believe* (Thomas Nelson: Nashville) 2003

Joel Warne: The Intimate Journey (www.wellspringliferesources.com)

Dallas Willard and Jan Johnson: *Renovation of the Heart in Daily Practice* (NavPress: Colorado Springs) 2006

Index of Articles

Thriving: Recover Your Life is an innovative and comprehensive life training program comprised of five different modules that will help you:

- learn skills to engage with God in order to grow spiritually.
- recover from painful addictions, trauma and attachment pain.
- learn to create community and healthy relationships around you.
- discover how to experience the presence of God in a way that heals.
- experience how God can heal the barriers that we have in our relationships.

Restarting:

Restarting is an entry module for the Thriving: Recover Your Life training. Through 12 sessions in Restarting groups, you will learn how you are created for joy. You learn how to recognize where your brain lacks joy and how to connect with others in order to retrain your brain for joy! Restarting groups combine joy-building exercises, DVD teachings from Ed Khouri, and the Restarting workbook to help retrain your brain.

Forming:

Forming is also an entrance module in the Thriving: Recover Your Life training series, designed for people who want to grow their spiritual maturity by engaging at deeper levels with God. You will learn more about hearing God and finding your true identity in Christ. You will begin to see yourself through the eyes of heaven and recognize grace as an active force for transformation and change.

Belonging:

In your second module of the Thriving series, you will work in small groups to restore your ability to create a joyful place for others to belong with you. Belonging jump-starts your process of learning the 19 skills that build healthy relationships and strong emotional resilience. You learn to recognize when your brain's relational circuits are off, quiet your distress, and return to shalom and appreciation with your relational circuits active!

Healing:

Healing is the module where you can discover more about how to experience Jesus in the painful places of life. Jesus is the healer, and by the time participants get to this module, they have built up enough joy capacity to let Jesus do His work. We pursue inner healing in the safety of groups of 3 to 5 people, and begin each exercise with God in a joyful situation! This module will utilize the Immanuel Process developed in connection with Dr. Karl Lehman.

Loving:

Loving is the last module in the Thriving series, where you will take what you have learned in all the previous modules and apply it to your own relationships. You will take the joy and healing you have been developing into the relationships God has placed in your life. You will practice receiving and giving good things to the people you live with and love.